HD

HIEROGLYPHIC DEFINITIVES

Champollion's Formula

RICH AMENINHAT

PREFACE

This book's primary goal is to provide definitive resolution to many of the basic and some major misunderstandings and arguments surrounding Ancient Egyptian writing, Meṭu Neter/Medu Neder, and its spoken language, Ren Chem [Kem, Kemit, Khemit, Khamit...].

I use the "CH" in spelling of Chem or Chemit because of its linguistically historical value: Al<u>ch</u>emy (Canaanite/Arabic: Al <u>Ch</u>emi), <u>Ch</u>emical, <u>Ch</u>emistry, etc.

The latter words each specifically relate to the Southeast to Northeast African development of the greatest most detailed recorded civilization to ever exist. This is definitively verified and verifiable in the longevity and qualitative advancement of Chem and Ancient Sudan.

Like the "CH" (K sound etymology, historical development), Ren Chem has its etymological story to tell.

To date, the scientific process of getting at or at least near the vital essence of the language was developed by Jean-François Champollion in 1822 CE.

As documented in his own journal accounts, he used the interrelationship of Hieroglyphics, Hieratic (A stick figure form of Hieroglyphs), Demotics (A further reduction of Hieratic) and Coptic as his primary essential tools towards revealing the secrets of the *Ραⲱιⲧ* (*Rashīt in Coptic*), *Rosetta Stone.*

Some have wrongly stated that the Rashit Stone contains Greek writing and others refer to it as Ancient Greek writing; while Champollion, a master linguist, stated the final writing on the stone is Coptic.

My research and findings show definitively that Ancient Greek is at the very least developed from Hieratic, Demotic and Coptic; NOT Coptic coming from Greek as some in error deduced and today baselessly support. Ancient Greek language and culture is undeniably Ancient Egyptian based.

I trust Champollion's work and word. And I trust the bread crumb trail of linguistic history that retraces its development and seamlessly flows _up_ the Nile (**From the Northern Egyptian Delta**) south to Lake Nyanza (Present day Lake Victoria) Great Lake of Kenya, Uganda and Tanzania.

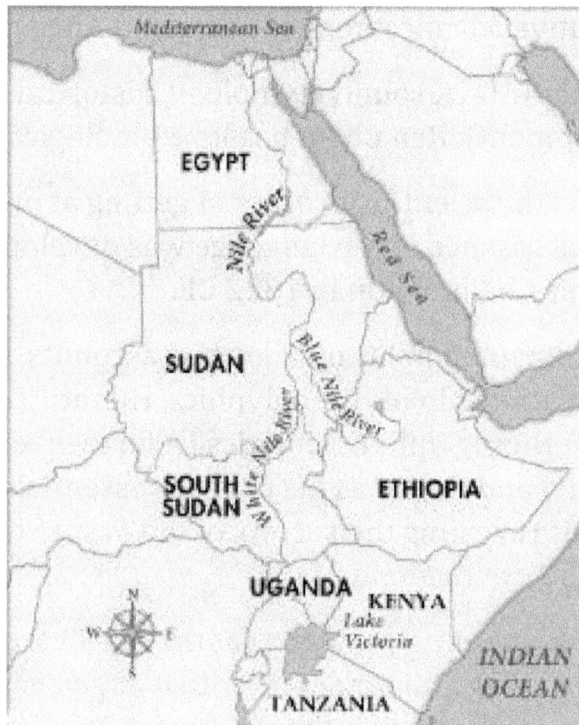

Thus in addition to Champollion's scientific work, I've added expertise in Ancient Egyptian Cultural Spiritual Cosmogony to create the ***Champollion Formula***™, for understanding the "inner and outer" workings of Hieroglyphics.

I dedicate this book to the Ancestral Lineage and Traditional Spirit of Afri Ka, Jean-François Champollion and my brilliantly darling daughter Kylene TiRaet.

Rich Ameninhat
HIEROGLYPHIC DEFINITIVES

CONTENT:

INTRODUCTION

[**BEFORE** the beginning, there was No Thing, not even a Word in the form of a thought... Thereafter; *At the beginning*, Supreme Being-Creator thought, spoke the thought, the Word; and All came into existence...]...

This idea is a reworked version of two infamously plagiarized "books" developed from the "Chem Creation Story."

The Ancient Egyptian *"Amen-Khepher-Ra"* Creation of the Universe story was written four – ten thousand or more years before the first borrowed, later stolen versions.

Borrowed, as Chem once openly shared its teachings. Stolen, as much plagiarism and active efforts to discredit the originators has taken place in national and international history books and academic institutions.

The more authoritative and original Amen Kheper Ra (The Hidden Coming into Being as Vitality) Creation speaks of No Thing, including not any thought, being in existence before Supreme Being/Nature/Neter evoking a "spell" upon itself; coming from Nothingness to "Neter one" to "Neter two" to "Neter three" to a multitudinous infinite amount of Being(s), Neteru.

The Ancient Egyptian term "Neter" has varied written and spoken forms, one of which adds a "ch" to the root form making it "Netcher;" additional to its plural or expanded form Neter-u (Neteru: Expansion of Neter from nothingness to many and all things, 0 to Infinity...).

Simply put Neter corresponds to "The Supreme Neuter, NEITHER this nor that," which is universally Neutral and thus ALL things, Netcheru, Nature.

As mentioned, the oldest records of this universal formula go back to 4000 BCE and have written and oral roots of traced existence as far back as 10,000 BCE, noted by the British Museum of Ancient Egyptian and Sudanese archaeology.

Relative to the "Chem Creation Story," the very first thought (Internal Utterance) is the basis for the very first speech (External Utterance), Uni Verse (One Verse), basis and creation of ALL.

This *Utterance(s)* in form of inner and outer speech in Chem is referred to as RA or RE. Thus Ra En Chem or Re En Chem translates as Utterance/Language of Chem and has a transliteration (Varied letters or spelling) as **Ren Chem**.

In accordance to Chem Cosmogony, All that exist, from the largest mountains to people to earthworms to the smallest grain of sand, has unique interconnectedness.

Each unique thing has its own personal qualities, vibration and energy that manifest as sound, its Ren.

Therefore another corresponding translation for the Ancient Egyptian word *Ren* is Name.

In Mandarin Chinese (Standard Chinese), Ren is one's Surname, familial usually last.

Renato (Re Nativity [Birth]) is an ancient Spiritual rites of passage of being **Ren**amed after entering spiritual/community Adulthood.

This is the basis for religious baptism and being renamed, having ones name changed "in God."

And of course Ren is the origin of the names Renate, Rene, Renée, etc. (*A Run [of Speech], Utterance*).

Yet with time, original meanings and purposes of rites of passage, community (common unity), adulthood and such things are often forgotten or altered in accidental or malicious ways. Meaningful purposefulness are lost or severely degraded.

Add to thousands of years of world-wide expanded use of Hieroglyphics, their evolutionary gradual changes, loss of their original meaning, some loss of "ANY" of their meaning, rediscovery of their basic meanings, theory and debate over their basic – original meanings and more; and the need for definitive (Definition based upon verifiable and verified solid information) understanding of Hieroglyphs becomes clearly important.

Life moves and the living who use language take words along the straight lines, triangles, squares, quadrangles and other various twists and turns life offers, including spirals.

With so many directions and much space and time it's easy to see how people, places and things can and do get lost.

Enter detectives to provide their highly practiced and developed ability of collecting facts, doing their best to piece together a plausible story backed by empirical, verifiable information to uncover the truth.

Of course some detectives are better than others. Some have natural tools of insight while others have to develop such skills. Honestly, some do not ever develop but have for whatever reason gained their profession and title.

From 0-10, ***best to worse***, most fluid to most densely stuck, open minded to habitually ignore-ant; detectives can be assessed and judged by their findings and ways of collecting them.

Linguistic, Archeological, Anthropological, Historical, Scientific and such detectives are of the same making, qualifications and rankings.

The greatest linguistic sleuth relative to Ancient Egyptian Hieroglyphics is none other than the Champ, Jean-François Champollion (Champ Ol Lion).

Not only are his findings unmatched by any of his time through to present, but also the manner in which he gained his verified information was superior and worthy of praise within any era.

December 1790 – 4 March 1832, Champollion le June (Junior or the Younger) of Figeac, France learned and excelled with French, English, Latin, Hebrew, Arabic, Syrian, Chaldean and Coptic.

Science, Archeology, Anthropology, History and more played a part in his personal development and study, but Language was a natural talent and love of his. He was a Linguistic Fo*ren*sic Scientist.

Above all it was his fluency in Coptic, a culturally and linguistically directly derived form of Ancient Egyptian; Northeast Africa, that gripped and led him to understand the Demotic, Hieratic and Hieroglyphic forms of writing from the same locales.

In fact the Coptic people, who were major founding contributors of the Christian movement from around 1500 BCE-300 CE, traditionally refer to themselves as ***Ni Rem En Kimi En Christianos*** (or Ne Rem En Kemi…, Ne Rem En Chemi…); and the direct ancestral lineage from which they came, Ancient Egyptians, as the ***Rem En Kimi***.

Exactly when the group of people from North Africa decided to label themselves as an offshoot or varied from the Ancients is not known, but their variation in cultural practices, developed language and new political institutions are traceable as far back as 2000-1500 BCE.

In fact, the Coptic people discussion is a perfect juncture to get into Hieroglyphic definitive(s).

The Hieroglyphic rendering of the sound "N" is established as being a wavy line, 〰〰〰 .

But how should one pronounce this glyph, eN or Ne [*ehN* or *Neh, as in* **En**ter *or* **Net**er]? How is it possible to know what the Ancient Egyptian scribe (Writing priest) was thinking and wanted to reproduce in sound? There is no simple answer, yet there is lingering evidence from BCE - CE to aid in solving this enigma.

No lackluster, lazy nor ignore-ant linguistic *hound* is good enough to honorably provide credible, potent, enduring clarification of this matter.

It takes nothing less than a very good to a super sleuth to do it justice and careful inquisitive painstaking readers to follow the discoveries for rewards of valuable revelations to be gained.

Starting with \\ , : , _ , ~, |, ‾ and a host of other symbols not often spoken of relative to Hieroglyphics is key.

These marks actually have their origin from Ancient Egyptian Hieroglyphs. There should be no great surprise as Hieroglyphics are nothing other than graphic representations of sounds and ideas.

\\ , : , _ , ~, |, ¯ and more of similar form and function are in the Common Era (CE), present times back to PEH (Pre-documented European History) referred to as **Diacritical Marks**; marks used to show accent, inflection (Exaggeration) of voice/sound, pause, "rolling of the tongue," and general sound variations.

In addition to Ancient Egypt garnering the first documented general and extended Alphabet, those ancient Africans were also the documented first to use diacritical (Distinguishing) marks; symbols that note differences in letters, words, sentences, paragraphs, and so forth.

In his 1957 book <u>Syntactic Structures</u>, acclaimed linguist Noam Chomsky made impacts in exploring syntax (structure of words and phrases) and semantics (meaning of words and phrases).

In English and the like, what would a sentence or phrase be without a comma (,) or period (.) and such? They'd be confusing or at the very least creating unwanted or unneeded room for varied, oftentimes wrong, interpretations.

Prior to and in line with Chomsky's ideologies, Swiss linguist Ferdinand De Saussure's 1916 contributory work looked at *Structural Linguistics* (Sounds of letters, words, phrases and their meaning).

It would be almost impossible to teach English (Anglo Saxon [Later Roman Empire Germanic]) and many other similar "Latin Based" languages without the use of diacritical marks related to distinguishing between sounds and language structure (Syntax and Semantics).

Yet for some reason between Middle and Present day English (***Old English used diacritical marks***), the use of distinguishing symbols mostly disappeared, making for confusion and varied pronunciation and interpretations of letters, words and phrases; creating greater loss of directly clear meaning in writing and speech.

In a similar manner, the use of diacritical marks mainly disappeared from Ancient Egyptian texts. There is no documented history that explains if this occurred due to general assumed familiarity of letters and words by scribes, foreign influence, laziness and other happenings, or combinations of all mentioned.

It happened!

In the introduction of Egyptian Hieroglyphic Dictionary, pages lxviii-lxix, Wallis Budge stated, "When they had invented or borrowed [From more ancient Africans] the art of writing, they were quick to perceive the advantage of adding to their pictures signs that which would help the eye of the reader, and convey to his [or her] mind an exact conception of what the writer intended to express."

Though there was a decline in usage of such "signs" or marks, the practice was passed on to the Coptic. On pages lvii-lviii of the same introduction he writes, "In transliterating ["Sounding out" of a letter or word] ∿∿∿ I have written *en* or *ne,* and there is good authority for doing so, namely the most ancient Coptic papyrus Codex of the Book of Deuteronomy..."

He continued: [**The letters with lines over them are an N and M**]

"Thus in ϩⲛ ⲡⲏⲉⲓ ⲛⲧⲉⲕⲙⲙⲛⲧ ϩⲙⲙϩⲁⲗ [A term written in Coptic] (Deut. 13, 10) the line over the ⲛⲥ and the ⲙⲙ proves that the reader had to supply some vowel when pronouncing these letters, either an A or an E, probably the latter. And this was the case with several other letters besides ⲛ and ⲙⲙ [N and M]..."

With all this in mind other ways to write Hieroglyphic N are I∿∿∿ and ∿∿∿I. The line before the ∿∿∿ denotes *eN* and the line after renders *Ne.* The line is a directive, not just a spacer, space saver; as some have wrongly deduced.

Additionally the line before the "N" hieroglyph can be placed above the wavy line to equal *eN* ∿∿∿ or below the wavy line, *Ne* ∿∿∿ ;

depending on which directions the Hieroglyphs are written (Remember Hieroglyphics can be written from left to right, up to down and vice versa).

Used <u>similarly</u> with variation in contemporary Coptic this is known as the *Jinkim* and resembles an accent mark or apostrophe, ('). In Ren Chem, this Glyph stands for *E*.

Case closed? Not quite... As in English, the Ancient Egyptian terms *eN* and *Ne* can have the same or different meaning from one another or with added hieroglyphic or general written context they have <u>various meanings from themselves</u>.

With English, *Enter* corresponds to "*In*" as in movement from outside to inside. Where as to *Enable* references "To make able"/endow/instill.

Conversely *Ne* is used to *ne*gate, make *Ne*gative (Ne, No, the Russian term *Nyet*, German term *Nine*). Whereas <u>*Nea*politans</u> refer to *Ne* as "*ne*w."

Like W. Budge wrote, the Ancient Egyptian writing used signs and symbols to give direct clues to the meaning of what the scribe wrote.

Thus the hieroglyphs ⌒〰〰〰 (Two conjoined arms with hands spread to the sides and the N) were used to show negation, leaving no doubt as to intentions.

With having knowledge of the hieroglyphic system, the Hieroglyph ＿ｎ＿ could be used alone to represent the negative and the sounds *eN (eNeN)* or *Ne.*

With the Glyph on its own, the idea of negation takes priority over a readers thoughts of how to transliterate (Spell in a different language or rendition) or say it. No matter how the linked arms and hands is spelled, "no means **NO**;" And of course *Jinkim* can be added for syntactical and semantic lucidity.

But without the added symbols to the primary *waved line hieroglyph* above, interpretation could vary between meanings: *In, to make able, of, from, not, without, not from, not of, not in, new, old, fresh, rotten*; depending on context. When there is little to no context, problems with discerning intended meaning arise.

With little written context the traditional Coptic name Ni Rem En Kemi (Ne Rem En Chemi or Ne Rem En Kimi) leads to further questions.

Did the Coptic people consider themselves separate *from* the Ancient Egyptian Rem Chemi? "Ne Rem" translates to Not Rem?

Was the difference in religious and political practice a developed part of the separation or were the Coptic actually *Not From* the same lineage of the ancients? Confusion, confusion, confusion...

If there was no historical information to help clarify the issue, linguistic understanding of Hieroglyphs and their influence on other "languages," including Coptic, <u>would</u> assist in setting the conflict to rest; giving definitive information to reveal the truth.

However it turns out the term Coptic is of Greek origin from Coptos and the related Arabic *Qift* aka *Qoft* aka *Quft*.

Surmised by some that the term Copt and Aigyptos/Aiguptos/Egypt/Gypt/Gyp came from the Chem phrase *Het Ka Ptah* (House of Twin Spirit Living as Ptah), the original phrasing is more likely **Het Gebtu** or **Gebtos (Gebt + [The Greek] -os)**, as confirmed by the "city" Gebtu, Chem being the very <u>*same location today known as Qift*</u>.

This shows with evolution of culture in Chem that the term ***<u>Copt</u>*** did not always connotatively refer to a type of religion, Christianity, but denoted is actual transliteration for the word Gypt/*Egypt/Coptos/Qift/Gebt,* a famous region in the area.

In fact, the Chem term **Geb** generally means earth, land, matter, material. The feminine form *Gebt* is from which the word Gebtos/Coptos/Gyptos/Egyptos/Egypt developed.

Relative to historical empiricism this example of *Coptos* is slightly compared to many of the unresolved issues related to the Ancient Egyptian Language's structure and meaning (syntax and semantics).

As Champollion "breathed life" back into the once dead Rosetta Stone, <u>Hieroglyphic Definitives</u> resuscitates the cultural, scientific, structural and semantic art of communication of the ancient hieroglyphs, not only to honor the past, but also to revive clearly communicated meaning relayed in present day language.

Without a healthy understanding of the founding past, there is great danger to repeat the same or make worse mistakes in the future. There is definitively no need to do so as betterment is present.

With this in mind and *Aquarian* amending energy, extents are taken to correct what has in error been used and institutionally supported in reference to the field of Linguistics and Egyptology.

One such issue is the use of the terms Phoneme, Phonics, Phonetics and such.

The labels are credited to Antoni Dufriche-Desgentes, an amateur self-proclaimed linguist who ascribed the Phoenicians as the originators of Alphabet and Writing given to Europeans.

He thus added their name as the standard of sounds related to Western languages and linguistics.

Not only did he muff with historical correctness, but also language wise the term Phoenicia has nothing to do with sound. Its actual translation means *Purple*, related to the purple dye and clothing for which people of that area famously exported.

Phoenicians no more gave Alphabet nor Writing to Europe than Christopher Colum. discovered America. And just as Columbus was taken out of History books for doing so and his National Holiday rescinded by some; so should the Phoenician historical debacle be amended.

Additionally prior to its Greek name, Phoenicia was referred to as Canaan. Prior to that name, it was called Kanana and earlier Retjen or Rethenu.

Remembering the location related to Phoenicia/Canaan is a main topic in the Chem story of "Sinuhe/Senuhe" (SĂ NEGT).

This story was written around 1990 BCE, 11 - 12th Dynasty, and many copies existed during the time of Amenemhat III in the 1800s BCE.

So called Phoenicia is dated as being firmly established users of Alphabet and Writing around 1500 - 1000 BCE, by then an afterthought for Ancient Egypt.

Thus in this book the terms related to Phoenicia and sound/language will not be used, along with exclusion of other historically improper labels wrongly institutionalized by "Western" Academia.

They will be replaced with more historically correct accredited honors given to Ancient Africa, including that of Ancient Egypt, Chem.

In the like manner, a Judaic fictional biblical account of "Races" stemming from Japheth, Shem Sem, and Ham fostered the concept of Shem-itic/Semitic (African-Asian Origin). Here the term semitic is devalued, de-capitalized, and mostly not used.

Firstly according to many Shem is not supposed to be at all African (Ham is the supposed paternal ancestor of all original Africans and some Asians).

Secondly, there is NO such thing as anything having an origin from Africa and Asia at the **SAME** time.

Thirdly, the bigoted racist ideologies of Japheth, Shem, and Ham have been historically and scientifically disproven of validity and proven as cultural and skin color bias and segregation as outlined in the Judaic Talmud, Torah, Christian Bible, Quran, and religious/cultural practices.

Lastly, Asia itself has scientifically been proven as having originated from "Africa" (Culture, language, people...).

To illustrate some of the Terrarium Orbis (literally Land Orb or Circle) aka T. O. shows how developing nations of lightest skinned Europeans thought about it from about 500 – 1400 CE.

Also referred to as the Orien Mare Oceanum ("Orientation of Sea and Ocean [around the linked land masses]) shows the then informally developed thinking that later would be nationally and intentionally formally institutionalized via Westernization biases:

Less formal and developed was a predecessor of the above mapping, which excluded the Sem (Shem), Lafeth (Japheth), nor Cham (Ham) religious propaganda:

The only true existence of anything semitic is a confabulatory, trumped up idea; at best an ignorant fairy tale and at worst a treacherous lie.

Not capitalizing the term is to call attention to its actually not authentic, less valuable, and certainly harmful nature, seen in who invented the concept, where, when, and why.

The truth of the origin of Alphabet remains to be seen here and further rightly spread around the world via schools and "word of mouth."

The truth flows from Ancient Egyptian Hieroglyphics and dialects.

CHAPTER 1:

Jean-François Champollion's Love Rashid; A What's Up?

No this is not a chapter about Jean-François Champollion and sexuality. Arabic *Rashid* or as it is written in Coptic: Ραϣιϯ (*Rashit*), *English: Rosetta, French: Rosette* refers to the Stone of Hieroglyphics and his love for his work.

Relayed in his 1806 journal he writes:

I am totally immersed in the language, in the coins, in the medals, in the monuments, in the sarcophagi, everything I can find, the tombs, the paintings, etc. about the Etruscan. Why? Because the Etruscans come from Egypt.

There's a conclusion that would make the academics climb the walls, those that have a smattering of Greek and Latin, but I have monumental truth.

I want to conduct deep continuing studies into this ancient nation. The enthusiasm which the description of their enormous monuments ignited me, the admiration which their power and knowledge filled me with, will grow with the new things I will acquire.

Of all the people that I love the most, I will confess that no one equals the [Ancient] Egyptians in my heart.

That someone so fond of the land and the ancient people would be the one to make sense of what others could not for thousands of years was no mistake.

Nor was it a miss take that he found the direct African link to the Etruscan, an Ancient Italian place located near the Swiss Alps, which boasted a major city called ***Raetia***.

Two hundred years later his words echo prophetically that the Etruscan and African connection would drive "Academia" mad.

And though Champollion showed irrefutable evidence, "they" still to this day refuse to amend their falsehood of Greece or Canaan/ Phoenicia being responsible for the Etruscan and other Indo-European languages.

No matter, because writing and dialect of Ancient Greece is basically Coptic and Coptic is directly Ancient Egyptian in form and meaning, syntax and semantics. Western historians are slowly coming around to this.

Further testimony to this is that for a documented twenty years and more, prior to Champollion's work, Greek linguists claimed to translate the bottom portion of the Rosetta Stone, but could not make one to one comparisons and translate the Demotic, Hieratic and Hieroglyphics of the same stone with the same ideas written in the four "different" scripts.

It took Champollion and his self-taught version of Coptic to correctly translate the bottom portion, thus make sense of all the rest.

Why do these truths drive "Academia" mad? Why, when education is taken so seriously at lauded Universities and scientific methods of proof and detailed findings are the standard, have the academic powerhouses not amended themselves?

It's quizzical, but more on *Champ Ol Lion*. About to become world renowned for doing what the supposed greatest minds from every academic nation could not, in the introduction of his book he "ripped" the arrogance and fraud related to ancient studies of the University system.

The book is:

Champollion le Jeune
Grammaire Egyptienne
Paris : Typographie de Firmin Didot
Freres, 1836

Though he was not alive when his previously stolen notes were reclaimed, Jean-François' fierce intellectual temperament and genius were retained in the publication made possible by his older brother Jacques Joseph Champollion-Figeac.

He had many critics before and after his groundbreaking findings, then death in 1832, but none could and can dispute that he did what others at the time deemed impossible.

Not only did he do it, he did it well enough that the grateful and ingrates could once again comprehend and enjoy the richness of the Ancient Egyptian-Sudan-Ethiopian-Kenyan, African lineage of Hieroglyphics.

Testimony from an admirer gives, "...Champollion became so expert in recognizing the correspondences between the scripts, that he would transcribe words, whose meaning he still did not know, back and forth from cursive [Hieratic and Demotic] to hieroglyph and from hieroglyph to cursive, until, like Coptic, it became second nature to him... " (The linguist and the emperor: Napoleon and Champollion's quest to decipher the Rosetta Stone, Daniel Meyerson, p 250).

"Going back and forth between them [Hieroglyphic, Heretic, Demotic, Coptic], he finally came to realize that all four forms of writing operated on the same principle" (Ibid).

Champollion wrote:

It is a complex system, a writing that is pictorial, symbolic and phonetic at one and the same time, in a single text, a single phrase and even in a single word. Each of these types of character aids in the notation of ideas by different means: It is a code (Myerson, p 264)

Meyerson gave an example of Champollion's transliterations, the Hieroglyphic *F (p 260):*

In linear hieroglyphics:

In hieratic: **ᕴ**

In demotic: **ᕴ**

In Coptic: **ϥ**

In an article for 21st CENTURY Winter 1999–2000, "Jean François Champollion And the True Story of Egypt," Muriel Mirak Weissbach cites a letter Jean-François wrote in 1809 to his brother:

> I have thrown myself into Coptic, I want to know [Ancient] Egyptian as well as I know French, because my great work on the Egyptian papyrus [hieroglyphics] will be based on this language. . . . My Coptic is moving along, and I find in it the greatest joy, because you have to think: to speak the language of my dear Amenhotep, Seth, Ramses, Thuthmos, is no small thing. . .

> As for Coptic, I do nothing else. I dream in Coptic. I do nothing but that, I dream only in Coptic, in Egyptian. . . . I am so Coptic, that for fun, I translate into Coptic everything that comes into my head. I speak Coptic all alone to myself (since no one else can understand me).

> This is the real way for me to put my pure Egyptian into my head. . . . In my view, Coptic is the most perfect, most rational language known.

His journal and his notes clearly show his method of analysis and synthesis to achieve his goal. It is obvious that in addition to wakeful work he took it to a dream state of meditative trance. That trance was further enriched by him talking aloud to himself in the African Coptic language.

As mentioned, the presumptuously correct conclusion that one could translate the fourth script of the Rashit Stone in order to translate and transliterate the other scripts was abandoned by most.

Yet Champollion's system worked. As with the *Scientific Method*, if one person can do it another using the same method and like materials will get the same successful results.

The British and other Westernized academic leaderships teach against the findings of Champollion's definitive work, but in the British museum arrogantly, type sarcastically put his work on display, as if to say, "Yeah... We are openly showing the truth that Champollion found complete usage of vowels and deciphering the Rosetta Stone via a formula critically based on Coptic to Hieroglyphics, but also in your face we will teach and propagate lies that Ancient Hieroglyphics had/have no vowels and the third writing on the Stone is Ancient Greek, not Coptic as Champollion stated and showed":

The French scholar Jean-François Champollion (1790–1832) then realised that hieroglyphs recorded the sound of the Egyptian language. This laid the foundations of our knowledge of ancient Egyptian language and culture. Champollion made a crucial step in understanding ancient Egyptian writing when he identified the hieroglyphs that were used to write the names of non-Egyptian rulers. He announced his discovery, which had been based on analysis of the Rosetta Stone and other texts, in a paper at the <u>Academie des Inscriptions et Belles Lettres</u> at Paris on Friday 27 September 1822.

Champollion's hieroglyphic hand (From Everything you ever wanted to know about the Rosetta Stone: British Museum).

And of course evidence from Champollion's own book:

28   GRAMMAIRE ÉGYPTIENNE, CHAP. II.

furent, comme les caractères *figuratifs* et les caractères *tropiques*, des images d'objets physiques, plus ou moins développées.

55. Le principe fondamental de la méthode *phonétique* consista à représenter une voix ou une articulation par l'imitation d'un objet physique dont le nom, en langue égyptienne parlée, avait pour *initiale* la voix ou l'articulation qu'il s'agissait de noter. Ainsi :

LE SIGNE,	REPRÉSENTANT,	NOMMÉ EN LANGUE PARLÉE,	AVAIT POUR VALEUR PHONÉTIQUE,	
🪶 ⌇	Une houpe de roseau,	ᴧкв. окв.	ᴧ . A o . O }	voyelles vagues.
	Un *aigle*,	ᴧᴦⱳⱳ.	ᴧ . A	voyelle vague.
	Un *champ*,	кóӏ.	к . K.	
	Une *coiffure égyptienne*,	кᴧᴧqт.	к . K.	
	Nycticorax,	ᴨотᴧᴧх.	ᴨ . M.	
	Une *bouche*,	рⱳ.	р . R.	
	Un *scarabée*,	өⱳрв.	ө . TH.	
	Un *œuf*,	соотᴦв.	c . S.	
	Une *main*,	тот.	т . T.	
	Une *lionne*,	ᴧᴧƂⱳ.	ᴧ . L.	
	Une *navette*,	ᴨᴧт.	ᴨ . N.	
	Un *bassin d'eau*,	ⱳꞵᴨ.	ⱳᴨ .SCH.	

56. Du principe phonétique ainsi posé, il résulta la faculté de représenter une même voix ou une même articulation par plusieurs caractères différents de forme comme de proportion. Ainsi, par exemple, un scribe égyptien, usant de cette latitude inhérente à la méthode phonétique, pouvait, à son choix, représenter indifféremment :

(*** In both of the preceding charts Champollion's accounting of vowels in Hieroglyphics is apparent and clear)

29

Though giving lip service testimony to Champollion's work, the British Museum contradicts him by calling the third writing on the stone Ancient Greek, though such writing preceded Ancient Greece, has a Hieroglyphic format without "Greek" grammar and accent marks like periods and capitalization, the exact type writing is historically found nowhere in Greece, etc., and the deciphered words ONLY make sense with the Hieroglyphics in the Coptic dialect, not Hellenes Greek, as Champollion confirmed.

The British Museum, thus government, falsely claiming the writing to be Ancient Greek:

[...]and 53 lines of Ancient Greek:

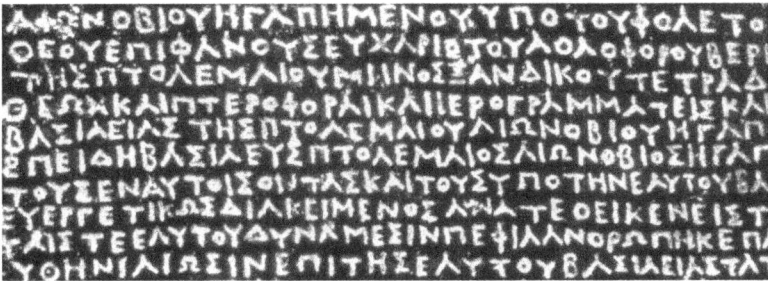

With all the Greek writing and speaking "masters" of that period, **NO ONE** was able to *make sense* of the third script until Champollion with his mastery of Coptic dialect.

There and elsewhere in Western or the like academia Ancient Greek means Pre- or Proto-

Hellenic Greek, that which is older writing and dialect of Greece.

In that sense Hieroglyphs can also be considered and called Ancient Greek, a tactic that helps blur historic accuracy and accreditation of "ABCs" and other such evolutions to African civilization, an overt goal of Westernization.

Thus a sample experiment, but with some ground rules applied to match the theme of this book, <u>Hieroglyphic Definitives</u>. They are (No necessarily fixed order):

I. A problem will be presented with two or more opposing sides
II. Definitive, factual observable solutions will be given
III. Supporting facts will be listed to support the definitive solutions

One major conflict that arose was the transferring of the British Museum's director of Egyptian-Sudanese studies and findings from Sir Wallis Budge to Sir Allen Gardiner.

Seeing and aptly foreseeing, Budge makes the statement that the more people studied and came with new claims about Hieroglyphics the further from reality and came closer to the confounding of the academic field.

A few infamous/famous professional **confounders** (Not cofounders) of the Linguistic and thus inherently other parts of the Egyptology field are Gardiner himself (as notably debunked on several "major" contributions by Richard Parkinson – a known author and curator of the British Museum), Birch, De Sassy, Palin, A. Young, T. Young, Lepsius, Brugsch, Budge, Ashby, Rkhty Amen, Collier, Manley and more.

Specifically in the case of Rkhty Amen (a cofounder of ASCAC [Association for the Study of Classical African Civilizations], and generally of the others, **HOW** in the world can you claim to understand the Universal principles of Maat, but passively or actively miss take that Jean François Champollion found NO vowels on the Rosetta Stone, that - that mistake qualifies the development of a made-up Linguistic Family (semitic) based on a mytho-religious story debunked by genetic science, then move to sell books and teach classes and lecture on such nonsense for elevated prices?

Where is the Universal Truth, Justice, Righteousness, Heart as Light as a Feather Balance in that?

If righteous, or at least objectively sound scholars, those people would come clean, make amends, and give Champollion and the Ancient African writing and dialects associated with Egyptology their due respect and credit.

More so a display of being off base, oddly Ms. Amen found vowels Y, E, and A to spell out her adopted Ancient Egyptian name.

Did such Ancient Egyptian words or names exist back then? How did she known which vowel to use where? If her knowledge or information was not objectively gained through study – on her African name – then how are the rest of her claims to be taken seriously without objective validation, especially in the case of vowel usage?

Another specific problem? Via studying Champollion, others and personal research, Budge stated that the hieroglyphic is a type Eagle, either Kite or War Eagle and has the sound "A" as in hat. Gardiner stated it is a vulture, is not a vowel and has the sound Ɜ, a guttural space holder; and many errantly sided/side and still support Gardiner.

Definitive resolution? The bird is an African Eagle, Crowned War Eagle.

1. The old and present day Coptic word for Eagle is Axoum or Axūm/Akhoum/Alhoum, **the name of the Coptic letter A**

2. The Ancient Egyptian word for Eagle is A-x-um [A-khs-oom], Akhsum...

3. The old to provincial Latin word for Eagle is Aigla and Aquila [Akhila]

4. The Chem term related to Vultures is Mūt (Moot), due to the Vulture's MūtHer (Mothering) care with which she protects her young [If the 🦅 glyph was an Egyptian Vulture, it would likely in Universal alignment have a "Mu" sound in connection with Mūt, as opposed to *A* as in hat

Do today's Coptic speakers speak like the Ancient Egyptians? No one knows. But they are the closest defined observable example that the world has.

To be honest, various Coptic speakers from different locales and sects do not all sound the same, have varied pronunciations and nuances. The point is to do our best with provable sensible material which we have to work.

Another issue with Gardiner's stance is the attempt to exclude vowels to match his theories. Most of Gardiner's differences from Budge rest in theoretical jargon. Because Budge covered and wrote so much information on Chem, Gardiner had to come up with something new to sell books, right.

Truth is there are vowels in every sound or grapheme, the smallest unit of a word. Whether it is written or not, is represented by a symbol other than the most usual form and has a click or guttural twist added to it; it still contains a vowel sound and is a vowel.

With making definitive the A as in hat sound, *Champollion's Formula* (CF), scientific method is used:

    A. Find a Coptic comparable letter

    B. Match the Coptic with Demotic

    C. Match the Demotic with the Hieratic

    D. Match the Hieratic with the Hieroglyphic

The process is complete when the Glyphs show a continuous closely related visual sameness in their progression, graduated development and meaning.

Additionally, the name of the letter helps complete the puzzle, and knowledge of the cultural Cosmology of Coptic and Chem is *very* helpful and at times a necessity; one many mishandle or miss altogether.

The next A as in Ämen [Ahmen] is a bit more challenging to define, because there is only one written A in the Coptic language.

This "A" (Ä and ä) is a reed and looks like this: . Knowledge of the Cosmology becomes necessary in figuring out the denoted (Actual notation or marking) and connoted (Cultural, societal or implied meaning).

In traditional Chem, EVERYTHING done by priests had specific purpose very close to a perfectionist degree.

With something as important as the invention of Alphabet, scientific precision of Left (Analysis), Right (Synthesis) and Corpus Callosum (Left and Right connections, intertwining and sharing) of Brain activity use was a must.

The female or male scribe had to have highly advanced meditative skills to access such.

With extreme degradation of the culture by 100 BCE, when confusion of Hieroglyphs which had once been known occurred, even those priests had to retain massive amounts of knowledge of the system from a spiritually scientific manner (metaphysics) to physics.

This is a reason why the Canaanite and eventual Arabic speaking people referred to Chem as Al Chemi (Alchemy) and the term Chemistry has etymological linkage as well.

Back on the case; is there a Demotic, Hieratic and Hieroglyphic progression of the same and similar (*samular*) shapes? There is. And how can the sound of the letter be derived?

Back to Chem priests being very precise and purposeful, each Hieroglyph has a specified shape, sound, natural function or other connection to the sound which it represents. It must *Make Sense*, be able to relate to the physical and metaphysical senses.

The Hieroglyph of a cat represents the sound Mau (Meow). A Hieroglyph for dog is Bau (Bow Wow). As Champollion noted in his studies, the system is deeply complex and naturalistically simple at the same time; like air, water, earth, fire.

With A as in hat, the shape of the bird body and head and the eagle squawk are enough to sensibly wrap up its form and function. With a reed, there is not the same luxury.

The shape and its progression to Coptic fit, but the sound a reed makes it not so easy to grasp. Meditative skills are a plus with resolving this. Meditation can bring one to the realization that reeds make sound when blowing in the wind.

Ahhhhhhhhh... That is refreshing. Thus a sensible connection is made to the structure of the letter fully drawn (Hieroglyph) to stick figure drawn (Hieratic, Demotic, Coptic and so forth), ∤ .

Ah as in Amen fits, especially when in Ren Chem Em Metu Neter Amen is spelled ∤ ▭ .

But also there is a *samular* Metu Neter ▭ . Would it make sense that the top glyph, the shoulder arm and hand, is one of the three "A" sounds? It does.

The rectangle with several lines sticking up is called Min/Men, a game that is the archetype of chess and was used as a meditative practice, an oracle and for enjoyment.

The highest meditative state in Chem Cosmogony is Amenet Amen (Female and Male polarities respectively).

Could this be a historical reason some people say the word Ahmen and others Aymen? Makes sense. And the "Shoulder" is used to make the Hieratic and Demotic and Coptic forms of A (Ā and ā), ▯ .

To sum up the case of the "A"s, we have A as in hat (A and a), A as in Amen (Ä and ä) and A as fate (Ā and ā).

With Medu Neder pictures, there is no need to guess which sound should be applied to A.

Additionally, like Coptic and Latin (Ancient Latin, Polis Laton [Senet]), all three of the Hieroglyphs translate as *To*, with minor differentiation.

Again the difference can be attained with cultural knowledge and form function of the Glyphs along with corresponding definitions of the terms by a noteworthy experienced scholar.

To, by flight or speed; *To, with subtlety silence or secretiveness;* *To, by walking as shoulder arm and hand alternate with the leg on "manual" travel;* samular to how in Russian the words *To Travel By Foot* (ИДТИ [Eedtee]) and *To Travel by Machine (*ЕХАТЬ [Yhot']*)* vary in form though linked in meaning.

Since in *Chem Cosmology* dual polarity is always an issue, the letter Glyphs mean *To* and they can also mean *From*, with the proper visual determinatives (Hieroglyphics) added to them.

A what's up? Definitively the "A"s have it, their proper placement and base contextual understanding.

CHAPTER 2: Ameninhat Hieroglyphic Chart

In just about every alphabet that follows the Ancient Egyptian, Coptic, Latin model the first two letters are A and B. They are in fact the two sounds that make up the word AlphaBet (In Latin-Greek: Alpha Beta).

Whereas the A's are soundly dealt with, next is the matter of B. However certain aspects of this letter raise more questions about *A* as well.

Prior to tackling this, the *Ameninhat Hieroglyphic Chart* (AHC/AHC [1]) can serve of major use in adding pictures worth hundreds of thousands of words.

Ameninhat Hieroglyphic Chart [1]

SESH MTU NTR 3500+ BCE / Hieroglyphics	SESH SHA 3200+ BCE / HIERATIC	SESH SHA II 2000+ BCE / DEMOTIC	Me NI REM CHEMI 1500+ BCE / COPTIC	U INE/HELLENE 750+ BCE / GREEK	L' ATIN/LATIN 1000+ BCE / ENGLISH
🦅	ࢁ	ࢁ	Ⲗ ⲁ	Α α	A a
L	L	♭	Β β	Β β	B b
⌐	⌐	Ɛ	C	Σ σ	C
⌒	∠	⌒	Λ ⲗ	Δ δ	D d
* ⎮	⎮	Jinkim ХІЇКШ	–/Є	Ε ε	E e
🐌	⌒	⌐	Ϥ ϥ	Φ φ	F f
⬚ or ⬛	⬚	Γ	Γ Ꝭ	Γ γ	G g
*1 ⏏	⏏	ᗡ	Ꝭ-Ꙅ	Ξ ξ	G-h
⚲	⌇	ᚭ	Ꙅ	Ξ ξ	H-h
‖‖	‖‖	‖‖	I̧	Ι ι	I i
⬌	⬎	⬉	Ⲭ	Υ υ	J j
◣	⩔	⩔	Κ	Κ	K k
🐊	⌐ or L	L	Λ	Λ λ	L l
🦅	⩔	⩔	Ⲙ ⲙ	Μ μ	M m
〰〰	〰	⁊	Ⲛ ⲛ	Ν ν	N n
℮	℮	℮	Ο	Ο	O
⬛	�III	⨅	Π π	Π π	P p
⌒	⌐	⌐	ϭ ϭ	Ϙ	Q q
⬭	⌐	⌐	Ρ ⲣ/Ꝑ	Ρ ρ	R r
⌐	⌐	Ɛ	Ꞓ ꞓ̄	Σ σ	S
⬚	⊤	T †	Τ τ†	Τ τ	T t
🦅	⌐	/	Υ γ	Ꙋ	U u
L🦅‖	L⌐‖	♭/∧	Β β	Β β	V
🐍	▽·Ꙅ or Ꙅ	Ꙅ	Ⱳ ⲱ	ω	W
⚱	⚲	⌐	Χ	Χ	X
Ψ	Ψ	Ψ	Η	Υ υ	Y y
Ψ	Ψ	Ψ	Υ γ	Υ υ	Y y
—	〰	〰	Ζ ᴢ	Ζ ζ	Z

To some the pictures speak for themselves. They show a continuous theme of the progression of Alphabet from Hieroglyphs (Fully drawn out pictures) to Script (Stick figure pictures).

One could say that as people got lazier, they drew pictures less; or as people traveled more and got busier, they needed quicker writing forms.

The historically true perspective may include both reasons, but more so has to do with the *Art of Writing* being passed on from **only** priests and royalty (Mandatory indoctrinated priests) to "Everyday people."

4000 BCE learning 3000 characters of Hieroglyphs and the art to draw them or etch them in stone, clay and wood was specifically relegated to priest scribes who pledge sincere loyalty to be educated in the skills learned.

Imagine having the best water, food, shelter, personal training, medicine, specialized training with adequate pay, in exchange for balanced doable services of national importance (Senet, senate?).

This tradition lasted strongly until around 2000 BCE when societal along with writing and general education standards had been relaxed due to natural ending of longevity, political and social strife within and outside of Chem, the decrease of highly skilled priests due to travel and employment opportunities elsewhere and such.

However the tradition of priests and royalty being the bulk of those who were able to read and write was maintained through and to passing Ancient Egyptian culture to Greeks, Romans, Hebrew and others.

Actually the concept of Universities was originally major *Cities* in which schools existed to study the *Universe*, Cosmology of this planet and others.

It is logical to assume that once Europe had its historical division between Church and State that state schools began to be established separate from the religious.

All of this occurred over periods of thousands of years. But keep in mind that in 2022, there is still a high world-wide illiteracy rate in general and in many cultures and countries women are not allowed to study at all, or are not allowed to study the academia that male students do.

To many in various nations and locales, the ability to read and write is severely taken for granted.

Even with those who value literacy, in school systems where the ***invention of writing*** is not in any way dealt with ***in detail***, people tend to take for granted the tremendous amount of wisdom, intellect, analysis and synthesis that went into developing the system that is Medu Neder.

Some thoughtlessly assume that the Metu Neter system began as arbitrary usage of sounds later recorded piece by piece and forced into order to make sense.

One of the most praiseworthy observations by Linguistic Egyptologist Alan Gardiner is that "The hieroglyphs live on within Western [and Eastern] alphabets."

The *Ameninhat Hieroglyphic Chart* clearly shows the graduated progressions. There is no accident nor forced constriction with the letter formations looking alike, samular. If it does not fit...

Moreover the letters not only look alike, but for thousands of years retained their denoted meanings, as is the case with the article "*A*" and prefixes/suffixes *En* and *Ne*. And the linguistic linkage goes on from there.

Take for example the Hieroglyph for B. It is a calf leg and a foot . What is the etymology of the letter B?

Aligned with the malicious or ignore-ant tale that Hieroglyphics did and do not have *vowels* or *an alphabet*; many Western and Eastern academic institutions, and thus scholarly writings, go as far back as Phoenician, Greek, Latin and at times Sanskrit as **original** sources.

But 90 - 100% of the time they do not enter Chem nor any of Africa into the equation.

With *B* we have much of the same with etymological dictionaries rendering *B* as *Beta*, meaning house. The languages that are credited for its origin are usually Phoenician, Greek and Hebrew.

Mind that when we add Proto- to Phoenician, Greek and Hebrew each case means originating from Chem; so the dictionaries are *generally vaguely somewhat technically* correct.

But by not giving direct credit to Ancient Egypt the sources could also be considered inaccurately misleading, ignore-ant of Chemit contributions or if done purposely, lying by omission; purposely leaving out information for fraud.

Or perhaps there is no link with *Beta* (B) to Medu Neder? Once again *Champollion's Formula* comes in handy.

Coptic has a B (Bida) and it translates to meaning *House*. Demotic and Hieratic have a B, so Hieroglyphics must have a B. We need only find what the meaning of the Hieroglyphic B is.

⌡ ⌐ ⌐ ⌐ is a Hieroglyphic transliteration for *Beda (Beta), translation/transliteration Bida.* The last rectangle with a door like opening is a determinative and shows the term refers to a room or an abode, house.

In summary, Medu Neder has the archetype form from which later *stick figure drawings*, like *Bb*, were taken; but also it is the origin of the letters' meanings.

Albeit potent, that is just one of the powers encrusted within the AHC (Ameninhat Hieroglyphic Chart). The others are to be revealed throughout Hieroglyphic Definitives.

Another high point of the chart is the semantics of Hieroglyphs and the stick figure Glyphs themselves.

The term *Medu* "letter for letter" generally translates as **M**: *Of,* **E**: *Out of the "Hidden,"* **D**: *Nourishment,* **U**: *Extended* or *expanded*; thus *Out of the Hidden for Expanded Nourishment (Divine gifts).*

Neter and another derivative *Netcher* refer to the *potent neutrality of Nature,* Universality, Universal Divinity. As such the term is often referred to as Divine Words.

Parallel to this, **Hiero** means *High/Divine/Sacred* and **Glyph** means *Writing,* thus **Hieroglyph**: *High/Divine/Sacred Writing.*

It is thought of as High or Divine Writing not only for the intense study one needs to learn the entire system, but also because of the evocation of sensual alertness and understanding it instills in the reader.

With the basic concepts of *Beda,* add the *B* being a "Calf and foot" and relating it to a locale or abode. The letter comes alive with specific determinatives pointing to *where, with whom, how, why* and even *when* **a person is standing**.

Also for example add other Hieroglyphs to B like *A as in bate (*⌐⫞ ⎮ [Āb/Abe]: ***To be, To be standing, To be housed),* (⎮ ⌐⫞ [Bā/bae/bay]: *Be to/at,* **B**e standing to, **B**e housed to/at/in*...)* and understanding naturally sensually expands, exponentially with meditative, critical and general thought (Note: Meditative thought is built into the Medu Neder system via visual/sensual stimulation).

No wonder the system excited Champollion so much. For those who can digest it, its nourishment is revitalizing.

Lastly perhaps not so easily apparent; with the *fully drawn pictures* the quickness and intensity of learning is greatly increased.

Those who memorize the AHC chart 1 will have gained the base fundaments for reading, writing and speaking the six dialects/languages displayed.

Also as language acquisition is cumulative, it will assist with the learning and usage of other languages.

CHAPTER 3: C the Connections

The next letter to be dealt with on the chart is C. It is not so much a Hieroglyph that has conflict surrounding it as much as it is a letter that has little use in other systems and hieroglyphic charts, in that the Glyph is redundant in sound representation.

As the *Ameninhat Hieroglyphic Chart* is arranged in accordance with the Standard English alphabet, there is a need to account for the letter. Doing so aids in the education process for those familiar with that format, and serves as recognition to how influential English is world-wide.

One vital connection C has is its sameness in pronunciation with S. C as in *PrinCessa* fits the build. With Medu Neder relative to scientific precision, a Hieroglyph has only one sound for which it is responsible.

ſ	ſ	Ɛ	C	Σσ	c

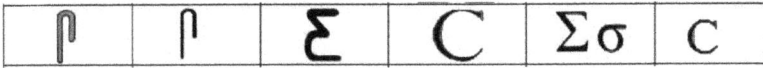

Like people in the world some Glyphs may look similar but each individual one has specified meaning and a specific purpose.

With the *Standard English* alphabet, glyph specificity is not so exact. Easily Prin_S_essa can be spelled with the S without any change in sound.

Yet in all practical purposes there is no need for there to be two letters that have the same sound. It is more a matter of linguistic evolution or degradation within the language why that occurred.

Why would S be given preference over the C glyph? Because S is more sensually connected with the original Hieroglyph form in appearance and cultural validity.

With the Metu Neter, the sound is represented by what some call a *cane* and others a *chair cloth* padding placed on royal thrones, aligned with the spine and featured in most every royal sitting pose, ∏.

Definitive resources to soundly identify the identity of the full picture letter comes from Chem culture, specifically the art.

Whereas canes were not of any unique importance, the "padding clothe" of royal

seats/thrones is often though subtly featured in
Ancient Egyptian art. With that, this author settled
with the Hieroglyph being a chair padding cloth:

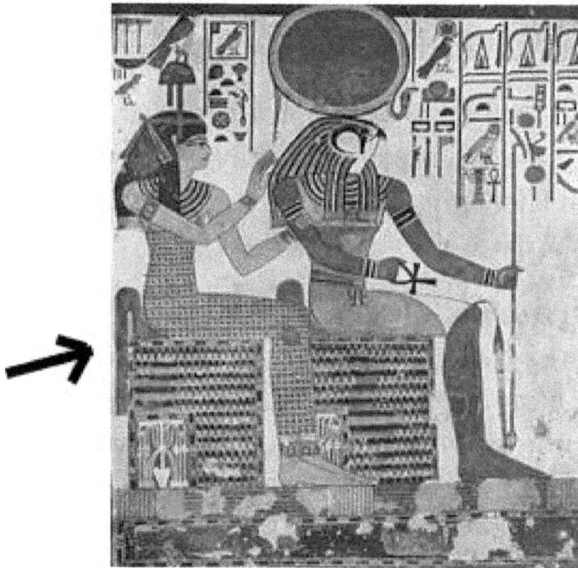

Verbal support of this idea is that in Rem Chem a term for <u>seat</u> is <u>*seat,*</u> for set, *set*/Set and sit for *sit*; all beginning with the S letter and sound.

To create the letter C the top of the Hieroglyph is cut off and then turned sideways:

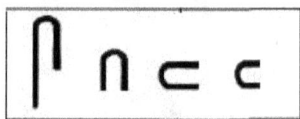

Π Π ⊂ ⊂

To make the S the bottom end of the Glyph is bent backwards to a comparable curve of the top:

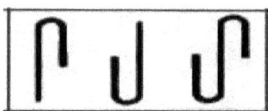

Π ∪ ∿

The Chem term Π as S' or Se refers to essence. 'S or Es refers to ***A call, calling or hailing***.

Related to its *Sonic* value, this letter in Coptic is named *Sima, Sigma in Greek*.

CHAPTER 4: D Wins

⌓, a loaf of bread is alternately referred to by some as D and others T. At the crux of this conflict Sir Alan Gardiner once again finds himself a major culprit, but is not the only scholar who has assisted in confounding the Ancient Egyptian written and spoken language.

With no attention paid to Champollion's system of identifying, transliterating and translating the hieroglyphics, Gardiner with theory upon theory chose a glyph that has a little connection in form and meaning to ⌓ , which turned sideways is D.

He assigned the letter T to the *Loaf of Bread* hieroglyph, which at one point in Ancient Egypt more than likely was used for such, in correspondence to being a suffix article related to femininity, though it is not clear is when this development in Ren Chem took place.

What is known is that in Chem ⌒ and 𝕯 ,

Hot Bread (Bread with heat flowing up under it) were used during **some** same periods.

In his <u>Egyptian Dictionary</u>, Wallis Budge explained the different Hieroglyphs as being interchangeable, while Gardiner omits the "Hot bread" usage.

This author:

1. Recognizes the similarities in usage of D and T (Ex: Tao [Pronounced Dao])

2. Sees it as unlikely priests of *Traditional Chem* would be wasteful and confusingly redundant to use one Glyph to represent different or same sounds

3. Sees a difference between bread and hot bread 𝕯

4. Notes the crossing T shape that is in the middle of the *Hot Bread* Hieroglyph

5. Notes the T shape fits the graduated comparison from Hieroglyph to Coptic T

For the above reasons and more ⌓ is assigned to D and 𝟩 is given to T.

D's Coptic name is **Dalda**, which further gives clarity to its intended usage related to its form. In Greek it is called **Delta**.

The **T** in both Coptic and Greek is referred to as **Tau**; a remnant of its historical connection from Chem, Raet **Tau**i (**Raet** Lady of "Two Lands," Yin and Yang, the Highest and Lowest...).

It may have been recognized that in relation to writing about the Hieroglyphics, at times the spelling Me*d*u Ne*d*er was used and others *Metu Neter*.

This is to illustrate how some people without any true purpose decide to spell the words with a D or a T, ignoring the fact that the Chem system is based on using variations of pictures to relay scientifically specific meanings.

This matters because we are dealing with **MATTER**. In the Universe all things have electromagnetic combinations that make them unique from any other person, place or thing. Each unique entity's energy vibrates at a coded frequency. Every frequency makes a sound.

All things have a person, a sound (**Son**-ar) that comes through and throughout (**Per**) its being.

Such is the Universal Law by which Mantra (Verbal sounds to invoke or evoke energy) are based.

Though not a huge difference exists between D and T sounds, it exists and is key relatively and at times specifically. If a situation, matter, requires the exact vibration of D; T will not be sufficient; and vice versa. Not theory but in fact, it *Matters* what one says and how they say it.

The writing compliment of Speech/Speaking requires *Spelling*. This is the reality behind wizards, warlocks, witches, priests, priestesses and people in general who cast *Spells*. If a Spell requires D, T will not work.

At its most fluently potent time of existence, Chem recorded and taught this Law in the form and rites of passage stories of Raet (Yin conservation = memory, **writing**) and Ra (Yang expression = conversation, **speech**).

When the rites of passage stories, priesthood and societal activities were altered from that of Amenet Amen Raet Ra Taui to Ausarian (Ausar Auset); <u>clear implementations of the writing system along with every aspect of Chem was degraded</u>.

To **not** understand the rites of passage Cosmogony of Raet in name or practice is to **not** comprehend the writing system of Ren Chem.

One of those vital aspects is **Not To Be Redundant**. Thus in the classical Ancient Egyptian language, different pictures did **Not** represent the same sounds and *different sounds were not attached to the same Glyphs* on a one to one basis.

When invented, Ren Chem was based on meditatively ascertaining the exact energy thus sound of a physical reality, thus gaining the appropriate symbol to represent that entity, its Ren.

Any person can prove this fact by working with Mantra and in and ex-periencing the truth that mantras provide. On its basic form this is called **Vibing**.

While mantra is generally considered a Sanskrit Hindi term, the Ancient Egyptian for Spells is *Hekau*, governed by the Cosmogony character *Heqt*; from which the metaphysical persona Hecate was created.

Heqt's numerical equivalent and hieroglyph is the frog/tad pole, testimony to the amphibian's ability to produce many offspring, reproduce various body parts and in general be a vibrational-*ly* virile Being.

Further why choose D to be represented by the *Bread Loaf* and *T Hot Bread*? Because the energetic vibration of Raet not only has Ra (Heat, Fire, Cooking) in it, but also has the universal principal of conservation (Bread) attached, making Raet the perfect archetype energy to correspond with ALL things *feminine* or *yin*. This is ultimate talking "Ying Yang."

Fast forward from 10,000+ - 5000 BCE when Chem language was invented to present day Common Era (CE) and the linguistic findings from then are still being used; so John (As in Johnny, Masculine) is complementary to Johnette or Johnetta/Johnnetta (His daughter, Feminine) and so forth.

A later development was to use A at the end of a word for feminine and E for masculine. For that to happen the letter E had to first be made into its present day symbol.

The *Ameninhat Hieroglyphic Chart* shows the Glyphs that would act as inspirations to the creation of E.

The truth of the matter is clear. Any languages tied to Ancient Greek and Latin thus Coptic are tied to the Ancient Egyptian Language.

Thus in essence and fact, they are not languages but dialects of their recorded most ancient version, Ren Chem Language and Metu Neter writing.

A child of specific parents does not lose its biological and essential link to its parents even if

it gets amnesia and changes its name, living location, gets adopted, or alters habits of dealing with itself and the world.

Such is the relationship between English, German, Spanish, Norwegian, Italian, Czechoslovakian, Armenian, French, Oromo, Amharic, Russian, Scottish, Indian (From India), Arabic, Hebrew, Greek, Coptic and more with their parent, perhaps Grand or Great-Grand parent, Ancient Egypt.

Definitive verification of this fact is first that each is etymologically linked to Medu Neter.

Also the dialects mentioned **Do Not** have any traceable records of their invention of alphabets or language, but do have actual history of developing into dialects linked to formally recognized establishment of nations.

None of the countries mentioned other than Ancient Egypt and Sudan, nor many others not mentioned but linked, teach the historical invention of an alphabet nor language; They CAN'T because those historical events and documentations do not exist and have never existed.

CHAPTER 5: Science of Silence

When a baby is born it makes *Every* vowel sound in human existence, no matter from what part of the earth or culture that child comes.

The new infant person does not have great control of its voice instruments thus the more difficult part of language, the consonants, are generally not pronounced.

Ancient African priests without doubt were familiar with child birth. With the meticulous nature they studied planets, stars, colors, dance, music, medicine, dentistry, embalming, yoga, wrestling, mantra, nature, death and more; it is difficult to believe the Chem priests did not pay huge amounts of attention to birth.

That is the very first time a human makes an external sound in the world and the event is doused with a cacophony and euphony of symphonic welcoming of life. As majestic as that is, the Chem priests had to have observed it closely.

With such and *hekau* in mind, they would have noticed the abundant base single, expanding double and combinations of vowels sounds; and consonants not so much present.

Linguistically, every culture and people that exists have the pool of same vowel sounds. They are unique consonants and variance in combining the basic sounds that distinguishes one language or dialect from another.

With careful attention to detail, the Ancient African priests would have learned this. With intense synthesis and analysis and advanced meditative prowess, they'd have tapped into the secrets of silence and building blocks of all sound encapsulated in it.

Via studying African Cosmology and Mysticism, Sigmund Freud developed ideas about the conscious and subconscious mind.

Yet by comprehending a working knowledge of those same universal models, he would have learned that the traditional African perspective is that ALL things are conscious. As such, there is nothing below or beneath consciousness.

The sub-conscious does not exist. The subconscious **subsists** as Nothingness in a state of

Amenet Amen, 0. From the Zero, there are infinite layers of consciousness, from celestial energy to seemingly meaningless rocks.

That air, water, rock and fire have consciousness is made clear in that they are oxygen, vitamins, minerals, light and warmth that give and sustain human life.

But not only re-<u>spir</u>ation is a key element to vivacity, also in-<u>spir</u>ation to feed the *Spirit*, the spiraling of *Universal Energy*.

Sound and language operate off of those same principles. Of these volumes of sounds there is one that is the most prominent, *E* as in *Exit*.

As a paradoxical statement the inventors/receivers of Metu Neter decided to at times exclude a significant pictorial visual representation of it.

The only obviously exact definitive form tracing of it from Coptic to Demotic is in **Jinkim**. However, such a pattern could be faked, fabricated, miss taken like the identifying of the Greek/Canaanite/ Phoenician/Hebrew "A" as in h<u>a</u>t from an eagle being morphed into a cow/ox, Aleth/Alpha.

The name of that A in Medu Neder is Akhsum, *A-khs-oom*, the Eagle. In Coptic it is *Akho[u]m*. In Latin it is *Akhila* and *Aigla*.

Yet when Letter A and term ***Aigeláda*** gets to Greece (Greek) it is turned upside down, slightly altered and thought to be an ox (⅄→ℛ→ϒ).

Thus the miss taken wrongly observed Coptic A is assumed to be a cow by the Greek and less ancient Canaanites, and Linguists and Historians retroactively, wrongly logged the Greek and Canaanite (Original Hebrew) letter as being an ox/cow.

Fabrication upon fabrication was made up to fill voluminous scores of books. Hundreds of thousands of lectures were given on the topic and the masses soaked it up while believing in the authors as scientific authorities sharing scientific authorship.

Here is a version of a chart representing the <u>false information</u>:

The Letter Aleph

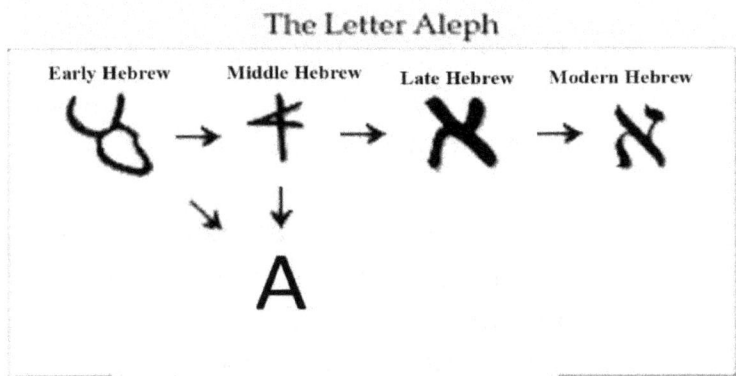

Early Hebrew	Middle Hebrew	Late Hebrew	Modern Hebrew

What is ignored, not known/shared, or lied about by purposely leaving out (Lie by omission) is:

1. *Early Hebrew* means *Canaanite Glyphs* that supposedly came from **Hieroglyphs**, Ancient Egypt, Africa.

2. *Middle Hebrew* is in reference to **Ancient Phoenicia/Canaan** (Named Phoenicia [Purple Place] by the Greeks)

3. *Late Hebrew* is from Pre-Israel (Israel was made by the United Nations after WW2, 1945 CE. That actual location Did Not exist prior) **Canaan**.

4. *Modern Hebrew* is a revamped version of **Late and Middle Canaan**

5. The Canaan alphabet is directly from Ancient Coptic (Ancient Egyptian) via Coptic from Demotic...

6. Heinrich Friedrich Wilhelm Gesenius, Gesenius, in <u>1813</u> showed the Hebrew alphabet's evolution from Ancient Canaan Glyphs (An extension of Hieroglyphs) through Middle to Modern Hebrew (See Gesenius' Hebrew alphabet chart below):

TABLE OF ALPHABETS

7. Gesenius' chart clearly shows that Canaanite, thus Ancient Hebrew, had the usage of written vowels

8. Pre or Proto Indo-European is in reference to Ancient Greece and Coptic

9. Ancient Coptic corresponds to 2000 – 3000 BCE, from Ancient Egyptian 5000 – 10, 000+ BCE

10. Hebrew, Canaanite/Phoenician, Arabic, Greek, Coptic, Latin are direct descendants of **Chem Alpha Bet**, a.k.a. Ahksum [Oxume] Beta/Akhum Bida/Alhoum Bida/Akhil Beta/etc.

All the while due to their preconceived notions, prejudice, for a thousand or more years the cornerstone of modern language went unused.

Lost until a true scientific linguist, a champion of a great lost art, Champ Ol Lion, Champollion used his evidently sound technique of Coptic to Demotic to Hieratic to Hieroglyphics as the basis for attaining success in grasping Ancient Egyptian writing.

With his solid method, Champollion found no "true E." Samuel Birch, who inherited Champollion's work in service of the British, found no true E.

Wallis Budge, a British cohort of Birch's, found "no identifiable E," but Jinkim, which likely stemmed from Champollion's work.

But when taking on the role with the British Museum following Budge, Gardiner with his arbitrary theories claimed Metu Neter to be Semitic (from mythology of Shem, of African-Asian origin) in form and cultivation yet erroneously fabricated an E from Hieroglyphs.

The culture and Glyphs of Chem themselves point to that which is the greatest being the smallest (Example: Most widely used sound being the least grand notation, close to zero, **|** [Jinkim, looking like a basic representation of one, 1] close to **0**).

Point being in Ancient Egyptian Hieroglyphics, though they were most definitely aware of the vital importance of the sound of the letter, physically/materially *E* had a small pictorial representation.

With the mistakenly identified Coptic A from Hieroglyphics to Latin the name and general spelling of the word Eagle was retained.

Once it got to the Greek (Just North of Chem by water) and Canaanite (Just East of Chem by connected land of Africa), usage of it was wrongly altered. This too tells a tale of the historical at times erred flow and development of language in this Present or Common Era.

As basic errors are observed and rectified in this book, there assuredly are others that need to be amended. When "listening to the dialogue of history," hearing well plays a great role. Best way to hear is to be quiet. That too speaks to the science of silence.

CHAPTER 6: Buh, Fuh, Vuh, U and Double U

When communicating, transferring information; unfortunately there enters "Chinese Whispers," "Russian Scandal," the game known in the United States as "Telephone..."

A person whispers a message in another's ear and that other repeats the message to another person and so forth, until the message has been passed around the room.

Seemingly 10 times out of 10 the original message is altered in some or many ways. At times the final oration is nowhere close to the original intent and form relayed.

Less organized is in everyday life when "Luke tells Rachel and she tells Timothy who speaks with

Makara, who shares with Rich, who illustrates to Mary, who expresses to Saul..." a situation that happened the other day.

Again seemingly 10x out of 10 the original form and intent of the message is changed.

Photographic memory is more often spoken of than *Audio-graphic,* and both are relatively rare, which lends to the odds of the relay of information being altered even when directly relayed from point "A to B."

Add to the mix of *Telephone* thousands of miles of travel and thousands of years passing in between the organic message and where, when and how the communication is received, and the odds for error are increased exponentially.

If not purposely done, the example of the Coptic A being turned upside down and mistakenly taken as being a cow instead of an eagle occurred with a relatively short distance between what is now Egypt and Sinai, and Egypt and Greece.

And with Coptic so closely related to Greek in form, the transfer seems to have occurred in a relatively short period of time, perhaps 1-3 hundred years as opposed to thousands.

This is why papyrus (Papyr-, Paper) was such a critical invention; Of course the term paper comes from papyr-us.

Those inventive personae figured out a way to transfer ideas with depending on a trustworthy person with a reliable memory and water resistant *paper* and coloring (Paint or ink) to withstand the journey and time; The oldest original paper/papyr found being around 6500 years-old.

As a region governed by Chem, the Canaan/Phoenician city of Gebal (Geb Al) was made to be a major exporter of papyrus to such nations as Greece.

The Greeks referred to papyrus as *biblos*, from Byblos; thus the rendering of the word *Books* as *Biblia,* from which the term bible comes.

To the confounding of word usage by the Greeks even with the best intentions and inventions, *Russian Scandal* occurred.

This most definitely is the case with dialects using the same parent language yet showing differences from one place or time to another.

Take for example Old vs Modern English from Chaucer's "Canterbury Tales" Prologue, lines 4-6:

"...The tendre croppes, and the yonge sonne[;] Hath in the Ram his halfe cours y-ronne, And smale fowles maken melodea..."

<u>Transliteration/Translation</u>: *...**The tender crops
and the young sun; Have run half the course of
Aries, And small flowers make melody...***

Now imagine that transliteration and
translation traveling through English (Anglo Saxon)
to Saxon (German) to French to Spanish to Turkish,
Armenian, Hindi, Italian, Canaanite, Roman Latin,
Greek, African Latin (Senet), Coptic, Demotic,
Hieratic and Hieroglyphics over a ten thousand
year period.

It becomes fairly easy to understand why
some dialects pronounce B, F and V, Buh - Fuh -
Vuh, differently.

In Spanish the term *Venir: To Come*, when
conjugated (Altered to match the I, You, He-She-It,
They, We, You [Plural] variations) is often
pronounced like a B; thus *Viente* (You come) sounds
like *Biente*.

In Russian, pronounced similar in English
Vodka is spelled **в**одка (Vodka} and *Water* as **в**оды
(Vodah).

In English, the term *Above* is often
pronounced as *Abuffe by some*. And the
interchanging of B, V, F rolls on from there.

The Ren Chem B has been maintained fairly
consistently throughout most conjoined dialects in

written form, but as seen with Spanish and Russian and other dialects it is at times spoken differently.

Russian, a Cyrillic dialect, is part of a family of dialects that linguists generally ascribe to Belarus, Bosnia and Herzegovina, Bulgaria, Kazakhstan, Kyrgyzstan, Macedonia, Mongolia, Montenegro, Serbia, Tajikistan, Ukraine, Chinese Dugan and more.

Viewing the *Ameninhat Hieroglyphic Chart* gives perspective of the former statement. Yet where Cyrillic and Russian are concerned the *Ameninhat Coptic to Russian Chart* (ACRC) serves better as follows:

COPTIC and RUSSIAN

COPTIC LETTERS	NAMES OF COPTIC LETTERS		"ENGLISH" PHONETIC VALUE	Russian Letters
Ⲁ	Alpha	Ⲁⲗⲫⲁ	a	А а (A)
Ⲃ	Bida	Ⲃⲓⲇⲁ	b	Б б (B)/Б в (V)
Ⲅ	Gamma	Ⲅⲁⲙⲙⲁ	g	Г г (G)
Ⲇ	Dalda	Ⲇⲁⲗⲇⲁ	d	Д д (D)
Ⲉ	Ei	Ⲉⲓ	e	Е е (E) Э э Ё ё (YO)(Ё)
Ⲍ	Zita	Ⲍⲓⲧⲁ	z	З з (Z)/Ж ж (ZH)
Ⲏ	Êta	Ⲏⲧⲁ	ê	Й й (Y)
Ⲑ	Thita	Ⲑⲓⲧⲁ	th	
Ⲓ	Iauta	Ⲓⲁⲩⲧⲁ	i	И и (I) Ы ы (Y) ь (-) ъ (')
Ⲕ	Kappa	Ⲕⲁⲡⲡⲁ	k	К к (K)
Ⲗ	Laula	Ⲗⲁⲩⲗⲁ	l	Л л (L)
Ⲙ	Mi	Ⲙⲓ	m	М м (M)
Ⲛ	Ni	Ⲛⲓ	n	Н н (N)
Ⲝ	Xi	Ⲝⲓ	x (ks)	
Ⲟ	O	Ⲟ	o	О о (O)
Ⲡ	Pi	Ⲡⲓ	p	П п (P)
Ⲣ	Ro	Ⲣⲟ	r	Р р (R)
Ⲥ	Sima	Ⲥⲓⲙⲁ	s	С с (S)
Ⲧ	Tau	Ⲧⲁⲩ	t	Т т (T)
Ⲩ	Ue	Ⲩⲉ	u, y	У у (U)
Ⲫ	Phi	Ⲫⲓ	ph	
Ⲭ	Chi	Ⲭⲓ	kh	Х х (KH)
Ⲯ	Psi	Ⲯⲓ	ps	Ц ц (TS)
Ⲱ	Au (Ô)	Ⲱⲩ	ô	Ю (YU or U) Я (YA or IA)
Ϣ	Shei	ϣⲉⲓ	sh	Ш ш (SH)
Ϥ	Fei	Ϥⲉⲓ	f	Ф ф (F)
Ϧ	Chei (Xei)	Ϧⲉⲓ	ch	Ч ч (CH)
Ϩ	Hori	Ϩⲟⲣⲓ	h	
Ϫ	Djandjia	Ϫⲁⲛϫⲓⲁ	dj	
Ϭ	Tchima	Ϭⲓⲙⲁ	tch	Щ щ (SHCH)
Ϯ	Ti	Ϯⲓ	ti (di)	

As with the Rosetta (Rashit) Stone, so called authoritative scholars and academic writings wrongly attribute Cyrillic to Greek, when it is <u>clearly</u> visible that Greek does not have as many same letter Glyphs that are found in Coptic and Russian.

While some attribute the erring to *Scientific Racism (*History and Science based on prejudiced bigoted perspectives*)*, it is just as likely due to ignore-ance at the highest levels of academia to the lowest.

Onward though, B is basically settled concerning V. V in comparison to U seems to be peppered with *Russian Scandal* and poor "Telephone" relay or reception. For resolution again we look to Champollion's Formula.

There is no Coptic V (B doubles as the V sound), which foreshadows there being no Hieroglyphic V. This is not to say that there is no sonic-V in the Coptic dialect and Chem Language, as the sound can be created with the written and verbal combinations of letters.

The AHC uses the [BUI] combination as a replacement for V, which uttered slowly is [Booi], yet stated quickly does justice to the wanted sound.

Yet deeper into the scandalous chaos, a look at the AHC shows the Hieroglyphic U degrades into the Coptic and Greek as a V/Y structure.

Historically that was how the U was first written in Coptic, Greek and their siblings, with a pointed instead of rounded bottom.

Again with a look at AHC, it is revealed that the Hieratic U retained its rounded bottom from the Metu Neter style, . For whatever reason the Demotic morphed into a forward slash, /. This in turn led to a conjoined backwards and forwards slash, \/, making V.

Once counted as the fifth vowel of Alphabet, it was adopted by Romans as the number five. And though named Roman numerals, the numbers are basic adaptations of Chem signs and numbers.

A close look at Rome shows they did their very best to imitate Ancient Egypt, from mythological stories to the infamous Roman Senate (Senet/Polis Laton/Esna) and creation of a city called Latin after the more original Laton.

And though considered a great empire, imperial Rome lasted from only 27 BCE – 1450 CE (1423 years, one dynasty?), a short span compared to its parent culture Chem.

Still Rome contributed greatly to world history, if only for the sake of mimicking thus keeping a fresh though askew memory of Ancient Egypt.

Notwithstanding, the V would **not** regain its rounded bottom until the 1600s with Middle English. Had the Romans copied Chem in a more astute manner from the Hieratic, they would have had it right all along.

Coinciding, that may have subtracted from the evolution of the Double U (Two Vs side by side, VV). Similar to V, W did not exist in Ren Chem as a Double U (VV). Its form is linked to a Hieroglyph thought by some unknowing to be a duplicate of U.

Testament, TestAment, TestAmen-t (A challenge or trial that is overcome via divine inner strength or external "miracle" and talked about or recorded for inspiration – testAmon-y) to this is also in the Spanish names and sounds of the letters U, V and W ([Yoo, Vee, Double Yoo])...

U is called and/or pronounced o͞o, as in You (Y<u>oo</u>).

Spanish for the letter V is Uve [Oovay], or Ve [Vay].

Lastly W in the Spanish dialect is called and said as Uve doble (V double[d]), Doble Uve (Double V), Doble Ve – Ve doble (Double V – V double[d]), or Doble U – U Doble (Double U – U double[d]...

Testament *even more so* that *We* are NOT speaking Spanish, French, German, etc., nor English **Language** (proper noun, capital L), but an ENGLISH, etc. dialect/language (small letter L, improper noun) that comes from an Ancient African dialect (Ancient Sudanese-Egyptian) closer towards the origin of the Language that gave birth to ABCs and all dialects associated with it;

It is a critical, key unification point for speakers of those dialects and expansions of theirs.

However aligned with Traditional Chem Cosmogony duplicates would be considered a waste. And for certain the baby chick matches the U form and its expansive sound.

Comparably, the lasso matches the visual "test" and at its Demotic style corresponds to the Coptic and Greek Double-U, W. The AHC aids in definitively establishing visual links.

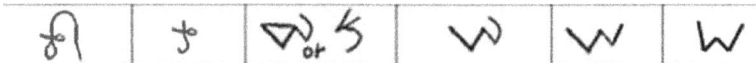

ϩ	ϫ	ⱳ or ϩ	ⱳ	ⱳ	W

With the linking of the Medu Neter (Fully drawn out pictures, for practical identification) with the Script (Stick figure drawing, more so abstract), the Ameninhat Hieroglyphic Chart is ideal for infants and adults, tapping into speed and enhanced learning techniques of the Ancients'.

CHAPTER 7: G House of Django

What should ring clear at this point is the recognition that not only does the *Champollion Formula* work, but also the names of letters are geared towards giving their *Sonic* value.

Add this to a comprehensive knowledge of Chem Cosmogony and culture, and certainties are assured with sincere carefully excelling study.

The CF works! With the letter G, it is perhaps the simplest task to align the Glyphs. Problems only arise when "Whispering," "Scandal" and "Telephonic" usage is matched by ignore-ance.

⊐ is a G! Its continuous etymological formation and meaningful content is succinct. The AHC wondrously shows its evolutionary simplicity. Its name is *Ghamma* in Coptic and *Gamma* in Greek, *Gimel* in Canaanite Hebrew and *Jim,* or North Africa *Gim,* in Arabic.

It has the sound as in *G*et and its meaning in Ren Chem, depending on determinatives, is: *House,*

To house, Heap, Pile, Hoard, Collect, Fruit, Fruitful, Greasy buildup, Storage, A room (All about material likenesses).

Some of the definitions in varied spellings are: ***Gh*** - *Greasy Buildup, To choke, Stoppage, Guttural*; ***Hh*** - *Divine of a Neteru/Netcheru* (Aspect of Nature) *of Eternal Substance*; and ***H***, the *Utters and belly, is Sanctuary, Place of Subsistence (Mentally, Physically, Spiritually with determinatives to point out what type)*; each varied from Bet, Beta, Bida and Beda, _stationary locations_ *of a person or people.*

Corresponding complements of it are guttural _Gh_et spelled with the ⬚ hieroglyph (An object holder [To hold incense, a cup, a head?]), guttural _Hh_et with the picture letter ⬚ (A Twisted Cord) and ⬚ (Animal belly, nipples, stomach) as in **_H_**et, and as a full drawn pictorial term for the word **_Het_**: ⬚ (Note: The Glyph and others like it are used "today" for masonry, carpentry and architecture to represent rooms, angles, mathematics).

Most often the G Hieroglyph, ⬚ , is drawn as ⬚ (A Corridor, room or other enclosed area), but remember Medu Neder can be written and read from right to left, left to right, up to down and down to up; with Hieroglyphs appearing inverse or converse depending on directional setting and the scribe's intent.

The arbitrary, unscientific, non-scribe like use of G, Gh, Hh and H is not only incorrect; but also shows disrespect to the *Divine Words* system powerfully and meticulously arranged for the purpose of clear deeply insightful communication.

How can one "say what they mean and mean what they say" if the actual words used themselves are jumbled and "confounded?"

Clarity begins with circumspection of the intent, purpose and factual meanings of the letters. With Ren Chem en Metu Neter, interpretation of syntax and semantics is concisely, accurately honed.

Lastly related to this **Het**, *store house grouping*, of Gamma/Gimel/Jîm is the J/Dj sound and Hieroglyph .

In his <u>Egyptian Hieroglyphic Dictionary</u>, Vol. II, Budge seemed to do his best to follow the *CF* by showing the Coptic parallels to letters and words he transliterated and translated.

However, when he got stumped he reverted to the Western Academician habitual practice of "fudging" the issue and moving on as if all is kosher.

Perhaps it is Academia's perverse "Leadership Training" that drowns honest work, especially when it comes to authorities, authors. Too often people are guided to fake perfection, never publicly admit wrongdoing, if ever at all, and put up an "air" of unbreakable continuity.

With such a standard, there is no room for admitting being at a loss of knowledge or information; instead "Act ignore-ant *to not knowing*, state your premise as if it is actual fact and deal with any collateral damage of your "front" by denying, eluding and denying some more."

Coincidentally this "Standard of Academics and Leadership" is the same tactic utilized by supposedly *lowlife* street con-women and men and church officials (I.e. pimps, priests and prostitutes).

Back to J/Dj, Budge presents the Hieroglyph

, a cobra like figure; stated that it is a snake that comes "out of" Ra; compared it to the Coptic letter *Djandjia, BUT* then labeled it with a **Tch** sound.

Ironically following Budge's summation, Gardiner uses part of the Champollion Formula and correctly comes to the conclusion that if corresponds to the Coptic Djandjia, then the snake must be the J/Dj Glyph.

Problem is that neither Budge nor Gardiner followed through with the CF and left their theories as foregone conclusions; both of which are heinously suspect, the usual criminals.

First off as the Ameninhat Hieroglyphic Chart shows, the J/Dj letter has a clearly defined physical link between the Metu Neter, Coptic and English renderings:

Secondly the name of the Coptic Glyph is **Djandj**ia, which shows sonic linkage to J/Dj.

Thirdly the related name *Django* translates as *To Be Awake* in Romany (Gypsy [Egypt, Qift, Quft, Copt...]. Aside; Why are "Gypsies" called Romany?).

Fourth, in Ren Chem, the terms *Djand and Djandj* (*Djandj-i* to show duality) translate as *To Experience, To Observe, Dangerous;* and lastly the name *DJ* means *Strong, Happy, Graceful* according to various "Baby Naming Books."

The J/Dj issue is settled with the correspondence of the Hieroglyph , a hand cuffed to receive or as if holding something to present, connotations of DJ. As the AHC shows via its glyph evolution, not only is the hand made up of a D form; but also a J.

Relative to the **Tch** saga, a bit of "fancy footwork" is required. First the general sound a snake makes is a hiss, spelled sonically *Sssssssss* or *Sz*.

Second, the Coptic letter that most closely resembles a hissing sound is Tsīma, *Tsheema, Tch*īma; pronounced differently in various regions.

Thirdly, the Cosmogonic relevance of the snake is that it corresponds to the Caduceus (Ka Duce-us [The Two from Ka]), the two snakes that correspond to Yin and Yang (Raet and Ra), rising up the Chem Tree of Life (Ka Ba Raet Ra).

Next, the snake Metu is translated as **Belonging to or being of the body**. And finally as the Caduceus or Uraeus (Ur R<u>ae</u>t Ra [us]) have to do with body energy centers or chakras (Cha Ka Ra-s or Tcha Ka Ra-s), the Ch becomes connotatively and denotatively wrapped up with the function of the Glyph yielding Tsh/Tsch/Tch.

Now obviously different from the Tch, the J or DJ are specified by determinatives, thus Hieroglyphic DJ with an added star, * , is distinct from Hieroglyphic J, , no star added.

That concludes the "G House of Django."

CHAPTER 8: Eye

Ameninhat Hieroglyphic Chart [2]

HIEROGLYPH	ENGLISH	*Corresponding general definitions* [Object Identification in Brackets]
𓆄	A	To, from, not, yes/affirmative (By flight, speedily) [Eagle, War]
𓃀	Bb	Stance, foundation, housing, storage (Material) [A foot]
Γ	C	Essence, offspring [Back cloth on a royal chair/seat/stool/throne]
⌒	Dd	Nourishment, female, of, from[Bread loaf]
ı	Ee	Exit, exist, substain, subsist [Small staight line]
⟋	Ff	Virility, male, golden ratio, father [Horned Viper]
🔲 or 🔲	Gg	Go, enter, exit, correspond [Corridor]
𓎬	Hh	Eternity, ancestral line-age [Twisted cord, DNA]
\\	Ii	Smallness, detailed, Iota [Two backwards slash marks]
⛝	J	Of importance, resilience, gifted, giving [Hand cupped]
◺	K	Raise, lower, exalted, decline, twin, stun' resemblance [90° Slope]
𓃭	Ll	The Article THE (Ex; Female: La, Male: El) [Lion front parts]
𓅓	Mm	Of, relating to, earthly derivatives, prey, pray, circumspect [Owl]
〰〰	Nn	Of, relating to, heavenly derivatives, evocation, invocation [Water]
◎	O	To/from/of Nothing, greatest potential/deficit [Spir-al, Rounded G]
▢	P	Belonging to, ownership, mine, material possesion[A Square mat]
☞	Qq	Who, whose, to/from/with... whom, belonging to [Cup/Kup/Qup]
○	Rr	Vital, flowing, energized, Divine Speech [A Mouth]
Γ	S	Essence, offspring [Back cloth on a royal chair/seat/stool/throne]
𓏏	Tt	Of, from (HEATED Nourishment) [Bread Loaf Fresh/Heated]
𓅱	Uu	Expansion, multitude, many [Quail chick]
𓃀\\	V	**Stance Expanded with Detail (Adopted as Roman number 5)**
𓎝	W	Expansion and Contraction, bring in or put out a lot [Lasso]
𓏴	X	Multiply, 1000, X out [Lotus or lily pad and root bundle]
Y	Y	Thee, thou, we, you, us [Support beam of the Universe]
⟿	Z	Close out, close in, zip up, zip [Door bolt]

The Ameninhat Hieroglyphic Chart [2] shows:

1. The direct written comparison of evolution (Etymologic development) of Hieroglyphs and English Standard Alphabet
2. The denoted (Of notation) general definitions of each Hieroglyph (*Note that for 6000 or more years the definitions of the hieroglyphic letters and English [Via Latin/Polis Laton] have basically remained unchanged; while there is greater variation in connoted [Socially defined] definitions)
3. Some connoted definition, often written within parentheses, ( )
4. The pictorial identification of each Hieroglyph in brackets, [ ]

Why is a picture worth thousands of words; Because it "makes sense." The senses (Seeing, Hearing, Touching, Smelling, Tasting, Balancing, Intuiting) are evoked or inspired to act.

Seeing is such a "taken for granted" sense. The eye is one of the most complex parts of the body and "machines" ever made. Its depths have not yet anywhere near fully been understood by Western Science.

External and internal visions (**Seeing**) spark **Sound** (Internal voices called thinking, emotions [balance]), **Smell** (Environmental awareness or lack and associated scents related to experiences with the objective picture), **Taste** (When smell is aroused the nasal ganglia [cells] connected to the mouth stimulates taste), **Touch** (Not only is energetic contact made between the visual object and the eye mechanism, but also the picture needs be relayed in an understanding arrangement. Failure to do so can cause actual physical imbalance, fainting or shock spells and other physically related actions), **Intuition** (Energetically "metaphysical" awareness, or its lack [Spiritual balance]) and **Electromagnetic** Invocation and evocation connections (psychic and physics).

A picture and its colors, texture, shading, complexity or simplicity of shape and more stimulate all of the senses at a very low to extremely high levels knowingly or unknowingly.

Metu Neter was created to take full advantage of communicating, with the senses in mind, in a way to have optimal comprehension between the writer and the reader. Jean François Champollion described it as being a "code."

The pictures have directly related and relatable meaning to the sounds they correspond. Additionally there are determinatives such as diacritical marks (Accents and such), additional pictorial clues or pointers (Placed at the end of a hieroglyphic word to give added context).

The former and the latter are meant to be arranged to fit within the Cosmological system of circumspection responsible for The Great Pyramids, Thousands of years of generally harmonious civilization, and of course one of the great wonders of the world often ***overlooked***, *AlphaBet.*

Not only was this writing system exclusively for the seeing (Not "blind"), but also because its raised letters were painted on papyrus, carved into tablets and walls and such; it had a tactile quality, like brail, that could be taught to those who did not have the full or any functioning of their eye organs.

As such, a person's other heightened/more depended upon senses could be activated via touch; for example some people who have visual impairment speak of more greatly relying on their "inner eye (A concept also used in regards to meditative practice)," sense of awareness, comprehension and intuition in order to make sense of their daily experiences or *in-spiriences.*

Whether an inner or outer eye is used for gaining reason to life situations, both are majestic and worthy of great intentional care. In deed such attentiveness increases the quality of life.

In fact, a Chem term for "The two eyes" is Ank-i or Ank-ti; written in hieroglyphs with two anks (Aunk cross, symbol of Life) side by side and two eyes side by side or one above the other.

Interestingly a term for "The two ears" is also Anki or Ankti, but with different determinatives pictorially added, two anks and two ears. That makes an apropos lead in to the linguistic etymological connection between the terms "Eye" and "Ear."

To start, *eage* (Old English Saxon), *aga* (Old Saxon), *ojo* (Spanish), *okw* or *aku* or *ocu* (Pre/Proto Indo-European); all mean *eye*. Some related terms in spelling and meaning are: eagle, eager, ogle (Stare), ocular (Of sight), occult (Hidden from sight), cult (An organization developed through specific training), cultivate, culture.

Then there are words generally linked to eyesight/eye/seeing yet literally are part of hearing/the ear: *Aura* (Atmosphere, ambience, air, quality, character, mood, feeling, feel, flavor, tone, tenor, vibe, vibration, sound... [*Auricular* (Of the ear/hearing), *Auricle* (Ear shaped object), *Oracle* (A message received, heard as in oration of an orator)]).

In Ren Chem, the term AURA or Aura means *Towards Expansion is Life Force* or *From "The Hidden (Amenet Amen)," Life Force Expands* and thus corresponds to ALL senses, as is alluded to in the general English definition of aura.

The simple explanation is that the more the senses of a person are engaged, the greater their interaction becomes. Greater interaction lends to greater quantity and potential quality of gaining valuable insight/comprehension/understanding.

The more meaningfully detailed a picture is the greater its inspiration. The system of Metu Neter was created to be used as a Quantum or Speed Learning tool and is useful as such presently.

With learning the Ameninhat Hieroglyphic Chart, a child or adult automatically learns 6 - 20 alphabet systems and basis for 6 - 20 dialects/languages, including all four directly Ancient Egyptian derived and any others that are Latin based.

Not only should the charts be studied intellectually, but also should be visualized in thought, shallow and deep meditation, before going to sleep, and in sleep; all of which are excellent learning techniques for any study.

There is so much physics and metaphysics to be spoken of related to the inner and outer eye. And just like the eyes' multifaceted complexities are often under or overlooked, that the word Eye has the same sound and physics and metaphysics connections to the letter and personal concept of *I* often lays ignored and *missed*, or not at all understood.

The development of *I* in relation to eyes was no accident. It was done purposefully and intentionally.

The saying, "The eyes are the window to the soul," comes to light. In Chem Cosmogony, the sun/sol (Latin, Spanish...) is an energetic correspondence to the spirit; thus the symbol ⊙ is used in relation to the sun, suns (stars) and Ra (Life Force, origin of stars and all).

That an eye itself has a circle (Iris) with a dot in the middle (Pupil) is an objective comparison, ◉. *Yet Universal Cosmogony is best suited to deal with analytical synthesis in conciliation with eye and I.*

In Chem Cosmology, separation of Neteru (All things expanded from Neter) from Neter/Netcher (The Supreme Neutral/Nature) is an illusion, a very critical one in fact. In Hindu and Vedic study the latter is referred to as *Maya Bija* (The Seed of Illusion).

It basically "boils down" to *All Things are Connected Parts of the Essential Original True Self* versus the idea that all people are separate individuals. Even the term Individual (In-divi-dual, The Not Divided Two) is recognition of Universality of Person and True Essential Self of Beings.

W.E.B. DuBois wrote about personal consciousness as parts of the totality of Universal "Collective Consciousness."

DuBois expounded that ALL things are part of consciousness, but only a small percentage of Beings are ***conscientious***, scientifically pragmatic with their consciousness.

Summation of this is the notion that *ALL that I see with my eyes is a part of me, I*; eye and I; I and I; II (The Not Divided Two).

For those polarized in segregated thinking, based on chemical imbalance of their bodies and brain, this concept is utterly ridiculously impossible and improbable.

However, they are not the standard upon which this book is based. Chem, Ancient Egypt, is the golden mean for this writing, and world; as no civilization has reached such heights since.

Imbalance though swings both ways. While one direction is bent on exclusion, the other is discombobulated with over inclusion. Some take the Ancient Egyptian teaching of Neter/Netcher and Neteru/Netcheru and create the philosophy, "I am God."

While their essential state of Being, essence, is God/Supreme Being; they personally obviously ARE NOT the active Creators of ALL that exists.

They are divine in essential quality, but not Omnipresent, Omniscient and Omnipotent in quantity; as is made evident by human limitations.

This present day error has its history as well. Perhaps one on the most infamous to date is the one where the initiate or priest declares "I am God," relative to invoking or evoking the powers of Zeus.

But in the ancient tongues it was spoken and transliterated as "Io Zeus," and "Je Zeus." Certainly this degraded into stories, personal relation (God is in me) and personification of Jesus.

Historically, it is quite clear to the sincere observer that the stories of Zeus, Io Zeus, Je Zeus and eventually Jesus came from the Chem Osiris/Ausar-es, Canaanite As**her**a and Asher**him**. ***Yet the original harmful intent of the Ausar rites of passage story has many times and ways often been disregarded***.

Factually, the original Ausar was Au Sa Ra and yet another way to explain personal and collective consciousness of an individual. Ironically, a symbol for AuSaRa is the "All Seeing Eye," a reminder to people that their essential state of being *Self* as I is Supreme Being.

Alas, the misrepresentation of the ancient rites of passage have eroded into people having conflict with being a person and having a supreme divinity about them as well.

Yet no one can sincerely truthfully deny that at times their life is governed by their personal limitations, and at others flowing to perfection as if divinely ordained.

Let this be a lesson that what one sees with their eyes is not the essence of I. Such a marvelous rite. It is transliterated into Ancient Egyptian Hieroglyphics as two backwards slash marks, \\.

From there it developed into one back slash,\, and later a slash made vertically straight with a line at its top and bottom, I. Akin to the vertical dash representing E in hieroglyphics, less is more relative to the formation of I.

At this point, the general link between eye and I should be unforgettably etched in memory. Please rehash the chapter and Neter rites stories for details.

The main clear conclusion why other students and educators of Hieroglyphics skip over the double slash as the archetype of present day I is the lack of consistent knowledgeable use of the Champollion Formula; furthering the clear definitive etymological and cosmological connections.

CHAPTER 9: 90°

At times scribed as ◺ and others as ◹ ,
with a curved line on the diagonal or hypotenuse;
this Glyph has a Coptic to Hieroglyphic, and vice
versa, *etymology* as being K.

In Coptic its name is **Kabba**. Its Greek name
is Kappa (*Note that the Bs in Ka**bb**a are upside
down Ps in Ka**pp**a/Bs are right side up Ps. This is a
link to *B* being used as a *P* in Arabic, and further
shows apparent mix-ups).

It has three sides in flat one dimension.
Adding three identical triangles to it renders ,
top view of a pyramid; , a version of a
Chem/Ethiopian cross; and ⊠ , a square like the
Muslim Kaaba or Kahba (Not accidentally related,
they coincide).

With the diagonally straight line the
Hieroglyph represents incline and decline in

general. The curved diagonal version corresponds to a slope or hill, incline and decline. What each keeps in common is the 90 degree angle.

By some; including Budge, Gardiner and Muata Ashby; this glyph is rendered as a *Q*. Being there are close similarities in the sonic (sound) equivalent of K and Q, it's not difficult to see how the two are interchanged or can be mistaken for one another.

However when it comes to the historical <u>name</u> of the Glyph related to the sound correspondence, its identity comes steadfastly into focus.

Additionally its developing from the Ancient Egyptian to Coptic (advanced and extended Greek) to English leaves little to the imagination of its written forms:

HIEROGLYPH	HIERATIC	DEMOTIC	COPTIC	GREEK	ENGLISH
△	↓	K	K	K	K

From a right triangle to a reorganized, juxtaposed right triangle the basic structure of this Hieroglyph has been retained for thousands of years, as is with most of the AlphaBet Glyphs including Q, seen in the AHC and explained in detail later.

Quite simply the right, 90°, angle of the triangle is moved here and there, back to front; whereas the diagonal straight line (hypotenuse) goes from being slanted, to drawn straight up and down, vertical.

Accordingly this *Divine Word/Letter* has direct links to the **Ahmesh Papyrus**, dated at about 1600 BCE and also known as the *Rhine Mathematical Papyrus*:

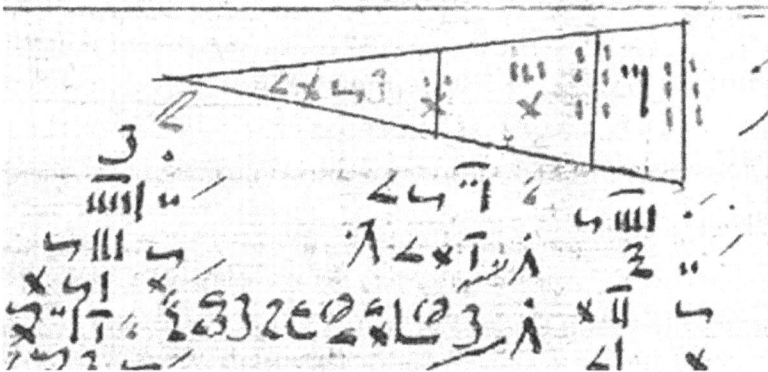

The previous small section of the Mathematic (Maat Em Maa -tic) Papyrus illustrates the use of a triangle, numerals and Demotic writing.

However, the construction of the Great Pyramids dated around 2600+ BCE shows advanced understanding of Mathematics a thousand years (10 – 40 generations) prior. Such structures would have been impossible to build without knowledge of 90° angles and their plumb alignment to the earth.

When a plumb line (A measuring tool of a piece of lead hanging from a string) is balanced, precisely vertical, its numeric value is zero, plumb. A connected or intersecting line to it at a 90° angle is called a *Right Angle* (Note *Raet* can be pronounced Rah-et or Rite, Write, Right).

Remember that before Champollion deciphered the *Rashit* (Rosetta) Stone some of the "great minds" of Europe designated the Hieroglyphs as "childlike scribbles," signs of an immature pagan civilization that wasted time on fantasy and inarticulate jargon of colored pictures with no trace of a communication nor writing system; never mind an alphabet.

Additionally to those "great minds," these keepers of the Great Pyramids (The Chem-au) could not have had any understanding of zero, the wheel, advanced physics, etc. and must have inherited the pyramids, buildings and all aspects of their advancement from extraterrestrial Beings and/or from a lost forgotten civilization that looked much different from them as being dark skinned Africans.

Turns out Champollion deciphered an alphabet and more, the origin of AlphaBet in Hieroglyphics.

Then Europe and "world" were able to read about the devices used to make the Great Pyramids (A wheel device was included), their advancements in poetry, pottery (Spinning wheel included), medicine, linguistics, beauty products, burial rites, astronomy and much more including Mathematical expertise.

This one Hieroglyph ◭ (K, KaBa, Kabba, Kahba...) set the foundation for it all. It is not only the mathematic counting prowess used, but also the Maat Em Maa principles which illustrate the basis of Universal Cosmogony, Divine Law.

These ideas were illustrated via KaBaRa (KaBaLa), the Descending and Ascending, Linear and Circular, Left and Right, and all directions of the flow of energetic life force. The system has commonly been assimilated as being the ***Tree of Life***.

Kabballah, KaBaLa, Kabala, KaBaRa, KaBa, Kabba, Kaaba, Kahba or other rendition of spelling does not take away from the valuable physical and metaphysical rites the Tree of Life has to offer.

Not having a circumspect understanding of the origin and multifaceted workings of the *Tree* is yet another issue and is where many rites of passage based cultures, societies, organizations, countries and individuals lack insight and proper application of Maat Em Maa Cosmogony.

Here is a sample of the system taken from Ancient Chem:

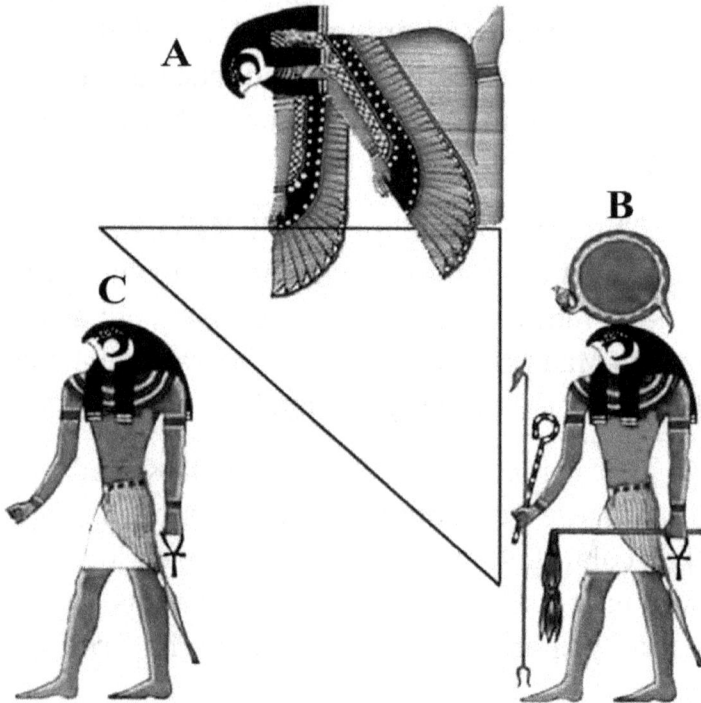

The picture shows what professor *Sadanand Nanjundiah* of Central Connecticut State University in 1988 termed *Jock Physics*, *Applied Physics* in its most specifically useful way.

On paper (Stagnant mathematics), 1+ 1 = 2; But in Maat Em Maa (Jock, Applied, Most useful, Living math) 1 + 1 = 3, or more... Meaning: A (The Mother) + B (The Father) = C (The son, daughter, twins, triplets, offspring);

[1] <u>One</u> entity combines with [2] <u>another</u> to create a [3] <u>unique whole other</u> individual Being or Beings.

The picture on the previous page shows A (Raet, Conservation of Life Force, Universal Ying, Mother...) + B (Ra, Expressive activation [Communication] of Life Force, Universal Yang, Father...) = C (HeRu, Managed coordination of Ying and Yang, Offspring). *He Raet/HeRaet + He Ra/ HeRa = HeRu (Heru)*, The Expansion of the Two.

The picture of the three Beings and the mathematic equivalence of the stories is the archetype basis for the Euclid, Thales and Pythagoras theorems recorded under Greco-Roman rulership 4 – 6000+ years *after* the creation of the rites and applied architectural and societal physics of Raet, Ra, HeRu.

When the rites stories were manipulated and bastardized with Raet extracted, the Maat Em Maa (Mathematic) applied societal physics in every way was maliciously also altered.

It was not just a matter of changing a story; it was the maligned altering of physical and metaphysical formulas used to maintain and better the quality of living for all who learned the application of the properties.

These facts give a clearer *spin* on the concept of doing wrong and "Doing Right." The general long lasting survival of the Great Pyramids are a testimony to them being done Raet; literally, figuratively and pun intended-*ly*.

The metaphysical and physical plumbing of the structures is unparalleled and remains an architectural wonder to the world, just as the fine tuning correctness of the entirety of the language of Chem has gone unrecognized for thousands of years as the basis of Alphabet; until now.

Respectful credit is due to Jean-François Champollion and others for their contributions, yet full recognition goes to our ancestors who devised the system of writing that has served well and survived from times of many lost records, 5000 – 10, 000+ BCE, to today.

Related to the Tree of Life rites here is a depiction of KaBaRa in one of its less pictorial, more linear forms:

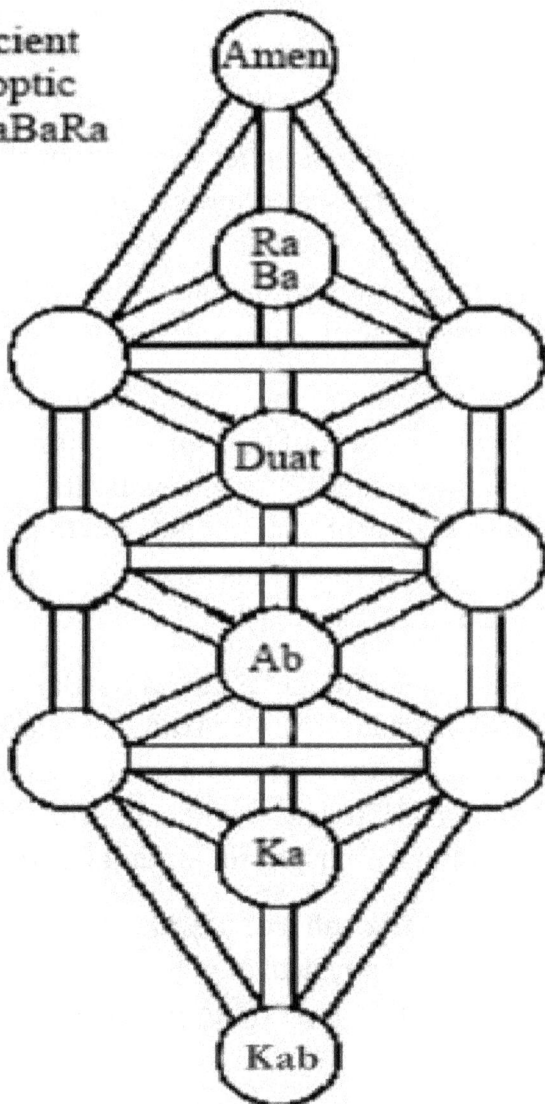

Ancient
Coptic
KaBaRa

Amen

Ra
Ba

Duat

Ab

Ka

Kab

Coptic is Coptic and its historical development. Ancient Coptic is Chem. This Ancient Coptic variation of the *Tree* reveals its full "12 Manner of Fruits," the 12 ciphers, and many of its corresponding line connections.

There are *right triangles* throughout the graph. The most extreme spheres at top and bottom, Amen (0) and Khab (10), correlate to the heights of metaphysics with a numerical value of zero and the densest physics, sphere 10, matter.

Aside from Ab, sphere 6, and Duat, 11, the abbreviation of the rest of the center column on the *Tree* is Ka Ba Ra (Ascension) and Ra Ba Ka (Descending) [See <u>Alphabetae Lives</u> by Rich Ameninhat or other resources for insight into Sphere 11, Duat].

Again it is no coincidence that KaBaRa spelled backwards is ArAbAk [Arabak, (Arabic)], an encoded nuance to the fact that Arabic is written and read from right to left and Metu Neter can be written and read from right to left and left to right.

Sum total, the spheres and the lines represent the metaphysical an<u>gels</u>, natural energetic personality types, and physical an<u>gles</u> (Physics) of the Universe and ALL in it.

There are infinite lessons and dictation that can be drawn from the latter. With his limited Eurocentric perspective, Gardiner did not only **not**

see the many cosmologic connections; but also he did not see how what he labeled the *Classical Period* of Chem, the Intermediate Period, was actually the decline of the Ancient Egyptian national and international external dominance.

The internal psychosocial reign of Ancient Egypt has not yet been nearly comprehended, never mind surpassed. When those days come, the use of the basic right triangle to make complex seemingly everlasting structures like the pyramids will return.

More importantly, world consciousness will have shifted away from inventing and making better *things* to the universally divine purpose of creating and maintaining the better and best person that people can be, conscientiously universal knowing of *Self*.

There in rests the literal and metaphorical rise and fall, decline and ascension of ◣ , KaBa/Kabba, K. The Coptic name and evolutionary structure of this Glyph link it directly to the Ancient Egyptian cosmologic Hieroglyph system.

As for Q it has a Coptic variation in name, Tshēma/Chēma/Qēma (Q as in Turquoise, which actually should **not** be pronounced as a K, but as Kw or Qu in Queen. Also the extreme variation in spelling and sounds show historical "collusion").

Hieroglyphically it is drawn as a cup, basket or bowl with a handle, ⌒; and when turned 90° clockwise its *Q q* form becomes evident: (.

The eating or filling of the bowl/cup/basket is left to whomever takes up the vessel. When one takes from or fills the item that person gains a knowledge, experiential information one way or the other.

All of this is linked to the query: [1]*who,* [2]*what,* [3]*when,* [4]*where,* [5]*why and* [6]*how* (5WH) of a matter which translated into Latin is [1]*qui,* [2]*quid,* [3]*quad,* [4]*qua,* [5]*quare and* [6]*quam*; akin to the Phoenician/Canaanite *Qoph,* Hebrew *Kof* and Ancient Greek, *Qoppa/Koppa* (Q).

It over time was dropped out of the Greek alphabet as a letter due to inter-redundancy usage with K, Kappa, yet was retained related to its numerical value of 90 (90°?, More redundancy or misguided usage?).

CHAPTER 10: The L Words

Lambdacism is connoted in meaning as **the inability to pronounce the L sound due to a medical condition, speech impediment or cultural acclimation**. It denotatively (of notation) refers to the Greek name for L, *Lambda*.

     Lallation is connoted as **saying the letter L as if it were an R, or vice versa**. Denoted it corresponds to the Coptic name for L, *Laulla/Laula/Lola/Lole/Laute/Lote* (The word varies from locale to locale).

     The connotation of lallation relates here as countless numbers of professional and novice linguists and Egyptologist since Champollion having vacillated on resolving the Hieroglyphic L in comparison to R, including: Birch, De Sassy, Palin, A. Young, T. Young, Lepsius, Brugsch, Budge, Gardiner, Ashby, Rkhty Amen, Collier, Manley and more.

The difficulty lays in various styles of writing being used over five to ten thousand years. Thus Pre-Dynastic writing differed greatly from that of 1500 BCE when Chem was openly accepting student priest scribes as well as being "forced" to educate foreigners from near and far nations.

However it is safe to say that Budge's translations and transliterations work well with his hieroglyph arrangement, Gardiner's with his, Amen's with hers, Ashby with his and so forth; Meaning they decipher the Hieroglyph's based on their personal understanding of Medu Neder, thus making/forcing the letters to fit at will, at times in line yet often adverse to the actual intended meanings, **without in depth reasonable explanation nor historical linkage**.

As with Budge, critical errors are made in not paying attention to Champollion's Formula, Chem Cosmogony and so on. With Budge he stated that L corresponds to ⟨lion glyph⟩ and R to ⟨mouth glyph⟩ , yet in his Egyptian Dictionary he wrote that either the sitting lion or the mouth can be used for the R sound and correlates both the Coptic *Laulla/Lola* (L) and *Rō/Ra* (R) with it.

His stance is just not factually so as the sounds are used independently within Coptic. Though they may be used to similar degrees within other dialects, the L and R most definitely are not used the same way in Coptic, Demotic, Hieratic nor Hieroglyphic.

If they were at one time used interchangeably with the original hieroglyphs or offshoot forms, this must be taken as a mistake and amended by educators and students.

As with the right angle, alteration of forms and substituting one for another is just not right and leads to linguistic, vibration and thus psychosocial error.

And though there are times when Champollion veered from his own formula, his stance was: ⟨glyph⟩ . Une *lionne*, ⲗⲁϐⲱ ⲗ L., for L a laying/resting lion (Young lion as there is no pronounced male lion mane), and an opened mouth for R, ⟨glyph⟩ Une *bouche*, ⲣⲱ ⲣ R..

In reading Champollion's *Grammaire Egyptienne* it is easy to see that his work was incomplete, due to a combination of overt and covert detractors and his "untimely" death.

Additionally, he was at a loss so to speak as the volumes of information that exist today were not at his disposal; He was the absolute spark of life to what would catch fire and become modern Ancient Egyptian Linguistics.

For the former and the latter and his overall success despite shortcomings, he most definitely is worthy of a pardon for his shifts from his own *CF*. In fact his incomplete work not only unveiled AlphaBet, but also seems to point to a *Hieroglyphic Syllabary* (Alphabet vowels paired with consonants system) from which more than likely the Oromo, Amharic, Ethiopic, Armenian and such dialect's alphabets come:

Amharic alphabet

	hoy		läwe		häwt		may		śawt		ra's		sat		ś		qaf		qat
U	hä	∧	lä	ሐ	ha	መ	mä	ሠ	śä	ረ	rä	ሰ	sä	ሸ	šä	ቀ	qä	ቈ	qua
ሁ	hu	ሉ	lu	ሑ	hu	ሙ	mu	ሡ	śu	ሩ	ru	ሱ	su	ሹ	šu	ቁ	qu		
ሂ	hi	ሊ	li	ሒ	hi	ሚ	mi	ሢ	śi	ሪ	ri	ሲ	si	ሺ	ši	ቂ	qi	ቊ	qui
ሃ	ha	ላ	la	ሓ	ha	ማ	ma	ሣ	śa	ራ	ra	ሳ	sa	ሻ	ša	ቃ	qa	ቋ	qua
ሄ	he	ሌ	le	ሔ	he	ሜ	me	ሤ	śe	ሬ	re	ሴ	se	ሼ	še	ቄ	qe	ቌ	que
ህ	hə/ə	ል	lə/ə	ሕ	hə/ə	ም	mə/ə	ሥ	śə/ə	ር	rə/ə	ስ	sə/ə	ሽ	šə/ə	ቅ	qə/ə	ቍ	qua
ሆ	ho	ሎ	lo	ሖ	ho	ሞ	mo	ሦ	śo	ሮ	ro	ሶ	so	ሾ	šo	ቆ	qo		

	bet		täwe		č̣		ḫärm				nähas		ñ		'ält				kaf	
በ	bä	ተ	ta	ቸ	čä	ኀ	ḫä	ኈ	ḫua	ነ	nä	ኘ	ñä	አ	'ä	ከ	kä	ኰ	kuä
ቡ	bu	ቱ	tu	ቹ	ču	ኁ	ḫu			ኑ	nu	ኙ	ñu	ኡ	'u	ኩ	ku		
ቢ	bi	ቲ	ti	ቺ	či	ኂ	ḫi	ኊ	ḫui	ኒ	ni	ኚ	ñi	ኢ	'i	ኪ	ki	ኲ	kui
ባ	ba	ታ	ta	ቻ	ča	ኃ	ḫa	ኋ	ḫua	ና	na	ኛ	ña	ኣ	'a	ካ	ka	ኳ	kua
ቤ	be	ቴ	te	ቼ	če	ኄ	ḫe	ኌ	ḫue	ኔ	ne	ኜ	ñe	ኤ	'e	ኬ	ke	ኴ	kue
ብ	bə/ə	ት	tə/ə	ች	čə/ə	ኅ	ḫə/ə	ኍ	ḫua	ን	nə/ə	ኝ	ñə/ə	እ	'ə/ə	ክ	kə/ə	ኵ	kue
ቦ	bo	ቶ	to	ቾ	čo	ኆ	ḫo			ኖ	no	ኞ	ño	ኦ	'o	ኮ	ko		

THE ARMENIAN ALPHABET

Ա ա	Բ բ	Գ գ	Դ դ	Ե ե	Զ q	Է է	Ը ը	Թ թ
ayb	ben	gēm	da	yech	za	eh	aht	tō
ah	*buh*	*guh*	*duh*	*ye(g)h*	*zu(g)h*	*eh* (not á)	*uh*	*tuh*

Ժ ժ	Ի ի	Լ լ	Խ խ	Ծ ծ	Կ կ	Հ h	Ձ ձ	Ղ η
zhe	ēnē	lyōn	xeh	cah	ken	ho	ja	ghad
zh	*ē*	*l*	*kh*	*ts*	*k*	*h*	*dz*	*rgh*

Ճ ճ	Մ մ	Յ յ	Ն ն	Շ շ	Ո ո	Չ չ	Պ պ	Ջ ջ
cheh	men	yi	new	sha	voh	cha	beh	jheh
ch/j	*m*	*y, h*	*n*	*sh*	*vō*	*ch'*	*b/p*	*jo*

Ռ ռ	Ս ս	Վ վ	Տ տ	Ր ր	Ց g	Ւ ւ	Փ փ	Ք f
ra	seh	vew	tyon	reh	tsō	hyon	piyr	keh
r	*s*	*v*	*t*	*r*	*ts*	*u*	*p'*	*k'*

Օ օ	Ֆ ֆ
oh	feh
ō	*f*

118

Though no one of note has taken up the task of exploring the latter, no detail will be devoted here as it is askew from the focus of this publication.

What has been explored is that at one time, like some "Asian languages," Ren Chem Em Medu Neder seemingly did not use the consonant L.

This is attested to by Budge and other Egyptologist Linguists, with Budge stating still Ren Chem is a purely African language and some others leaning towards it being an Oriental (Eastern)/ Asian or African-Asian Origin (*Semitic*, which does not actually exist. No language originated in Africa and Asia at the same time.).

Yet through the erudite work of such scholars as Ivan Van Sertima and Runoko Rashidi, world academia has been pushed to recognize that there is no such thing as an original African-Asian language, though some still cling to the idea and term and its outdated/antiquated usage.

In fact contemporary archaeology and genealogy point to Asian people and thus their cultures as being solely *African in origin* and the term and idea of semitic (Lower case S is warranted as the term is a failed theory and is not a proper noun) has been debunked and considered false *Scientific Racism*.

From the vantage of their advancements in science; anthropologists, archaeologists, genealogists and such in general side with the overwhelming evidence that all people, thus cultures originated from Africa.

Such findings make it commonsensical (Though not necessarily true) to state that Alphabet and all dialects *off-sprung* from it originated from Africa.

The rigorous and in depth study of Hieroglyphics yields empirically undeniable evidence that all Latin based languages stemmed from them.

Again this means that the so called languages: English, German, French, Spanish, Irish, Italian, Russian (Cyrillic), Ebonics and so on are no more than dialects of the Ancient Egyptian Language.

Too often academia and its devotees "thumb their nose" at the "Out of Africa" concept and relegate such studies as secondary to Eurocentric ideas, and purely Afri-centric buffoonery.

Nevertheless as scientific facts points to Africa as the ancestral birthplace of all humans, such infantile ignorance ought to be put to rest. This more mature and scientifically aligned sentiment is also expressed in Jean-François Champollion's work.

Back to the primary topic of definitive hieroglyphics, there is more to delve into relative to R.

HIEROGLYPH	HIERATIC	DEMOTIC	COPTIC	GREEK	ENGLISH
⬯	⎝	𝔻 or ⌐	P or ₽?	P	Rr

The above portion taken from the *Ameninhat Hieroglyphic Chart* shows the evolution of R.

Instantly a person only accustomed to Standard English and dialects like it should be perplexed that the Coptic and Greek glyphs for *Rō/Ra* look like a P.

Admittedly, there is an odd transformation from Hieroglyphic to Hieratic, yet they are somewhat in accord, with the left corners of the hieroglyphic mouth and the hieratic symbol retained.

The Demotic form of *Rō/Ra* is a bit more familiar as it bares close resemblance to the "Small letter" (r). But how does one get a R from P?

Then confusion strikes again. The Champollion Formula seems to be of no use for this letter. Fortunately despite preliminary doubt, there arrives a symbol written as a Coptic letter but without any name nor sound attached to it in its contemporary dialect, Ⲣ ⲣ.

Ⲣ ⲣ is the Coptic Glyph for the number 900. It is written along with the Standard Coptic alphabet, though at times ignore-antly excluded. The symbol is a cross between a P with a T added to its lower part.

When the head of the glyph is taken off it resembles a crude (r), ⲧ ⲧ, similar to that of the Demotic forms. And lastly with its horizontal line extracted and placed in front of it diagonally, it unmistakably shows as an R, R.

Add to this that Kabba/Kappa/△ corresponds to a right triangle of 90°; Qēma/Qoppa/Koppa/⌣ is the numerical equivalent of 90; Ⲣ ⲣ has no name nor sonic expression in Coptic, but is mathematically 900; and that R is rendered a P in Coptic; Greek; Russian and some others dialects, and it seems very clear that a "Chinese Whisper" through the "Telephone" created more "Russian Scandal," confusing the structures and meanings of glyphs from their original Hieroglyphic, Divine Words, intent.

But wait, there's more evidence. The Greek P sound is correlated to the glyph Pi, Π (3.14...). Akin to Pi is a glyph long removed from the Greek alphabet. It is called Sampi (Sam Pi), ⟆ . It is thought to be an evolution of the phrase San Pi (*Like Pi*).

It looks like a slanted Pi, thus Greco slanted P. Though its actual original sound is unknown, its numerical value is 900, like Coptic Ϥ ϥ. There most definitely were evolutionary mistakes made related to the glyphs and corresponding sounds R, P, ℼ, ⟆ and Ϥ ϥ.

Fixing these issues is a basic fundamentally correct thing to do, but admitting the wrong and <u>actually</u> making the necessary changes to properly align with the intended linguistically mathematic formula, the invention of Alphabet, is a whole other task.

Related to the Champollion Formula and the Ameninhat Hieroglyphic Chart, the Glyph Ϥ ϥ is an R, ⬥ , not a P; and P is a *Pee*. **Coptic and Russian (Cyrillic) linguists would be wise to follow suit and make amends.**

CHAPTER 11: Oh, No

When "historians" communicate that the zero, 0, was invented by Arabs (Origin around 6th Century, 501 – 600, CE/AD) they are either speaking out of ignorance or lying for whatever reason.

Without the concept and use of zero, the Ancient Egyptians could not have come up with the Cosmogony of Amenet Amen (Subjective Being of Nothingness from which all things come) around 6000 – 10,000 plus BCE.

Neither could they have constructed ANYTHING, never mind the Great Pyramids around 2600 BCE. There could be no scales for weighing market goods or "hearts."

The scales of Maat when at zero mean perfect balance between a feather and one's heart (Mind, Conscience). The cipher with a dot,⊙, in the middle speaks of well-focused attention in correspondence to Raet Ra (BA level of conscientiousness) or HeRu (Ab level of conscientiousness) from that of Raet Taui's Ka level of conscientiousness (Raet, ⊙ Ra, HeRu).

This Hieroglyph ⊙ is used (Over 6000 years of documented use) to this day in Astronomy, Astrology, Taro and more, representative of a star, a sun, the Sun in our *Solar* system.

It is telling that the often Hawk Headed Raet, Ra and Heru symbol used as a metaphor for Hawk-like physical and "mental" focus in the Eurocentric taxonomy is labeled a *bullseye*, related to shooting (Violence alluded) through the eye socket carcass skull of a not so smart animal, a bull.

Amended to the Divine Word intent, most original meaning of the symbol, the dot in the center of a circle refers to spiritual, mental and physical potent acuity.

Of course remove the dot from the center and you have O, 0 [Oh, Zero], a cipher; the cipher of Amenet Amen.

Oddly there are still people who argue that the Ancient Egyptians had no O, Oh, in their writing system.

They state that Metu Neter is an Abjad, a letter and writing arrangement that only uses consonants expecting the reader to provide the needed vowels, and has no vowels.

In contradiction the term Abjad or Abgad is derived from the order of the Coptic, Hebrew, Arabic and such alphabets where the first four letters historically were Alhoum, Bida, Gimma and Dalta/Alpha, Beta, Gamma, and Delta (ABG[a]D/abj[a]d). Notably the first A is present in writing the word abjad though the second A must be added.

Though at times excluded in written form, clearly vowels existed and exist in the Arabic, Hebrew and Coptic; as did they exist with Demotic, Hieratic and Hieroglyphic. NO spoken lingua can exist without vowels.

Not only does the Ra en Chem and Metu Neter have vowels; but also it contains a Syllabary, Di-Syllabary (2 letter combination of consonant and vowel), Tri-Syllabary (3 letters of consonants and vowel) and perhaps more formats.

In fact the term *Di* (Dual) comes directly from the Ancient Egyptian ⌂Y, or ⌂ (In the Budge system, which also stands for *Tï*).

In the Ameninhat Hieroglyphic Definitive System (AHDS) *Tī is* 𝕯𝕐, leaving no guessing for the reader of the scribe's original intent.

With the Budge and others' Hieroglyphic spelling, there is no way for the reader on their own to differentiate between Di, Dī, Ti and Tī, leaving the hieroglyphic writing up to arbitrary interpretation.

Though the Gardiner system claims Hieroglyphics is without vowels, he showed and used hieroglyphic vowels and simply used glyphs such as ['] to represent vowels that Budge used glyphs of A, E, I, O, U, Y in his transliterations and translations. Gardiner, as some still do with Hieroglyphs, contradicted himself in the vowel issue as well as in other regards.

Is Medu Neter an "Abjad?" No. Are there vowels in Medu Neter? Yes. Was there an O and 0 [Oh and Zero] in Metu Neter? Yes, of course... In the markets, pyramid building, writing and cosmologic system, linked as one!

As mentioned previously, human babes make all vowel and combinations of vowel sounds possible when born. Consonants are learned and developed.

The sonic O is no exception and thus was known by the people of Chem. Keeping with the mode of not being wastefully redundant, the spiral cord (◎ Glyph is the "alive center" perfect structure for its etymological lineage.

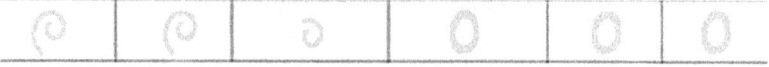

◎	◎	◑	0	0	0

When the central portion of the spiral is isolated and closed, the cipher form is made.

The spiral [Spir Ra El] is in so many ways linked to evolving and revolving life and life cycles from RNA and DNA strands; to motions, Fibonacci patterns of plants; the terms Spirit, Inspiration, Expiration; hair; fingerprints; wind/air; solar systems and galaxies; and so on.

That it is also referred to as a _helix_ is yet another correspondence to sun centered (_heliocentric_) formations and ideas, life giving and maintaining properties.

Specifically in Irish the term O means descendant (Ex: O'Hara – Descendant of Hara, etc.). Type O Rh D negative blood is considered Universal, where O positive is the most common. _Cipher/Cypher/Cifer/Cifre/Cifra/Sephira/Sifr/ Safara/Sa Fa Ra_ are various forms from several dialects/so called languages with a common root value and meaning.

In Ren Chem **Sa Fa Ra** is generally translated as **Essence Yang Potency of Ra**.

In Sanskrit it is used in relation to movement (Safari) and emptiness (Zira, Zero...). The terms origins and conceptual correlations are as ancient as the Hieroglyph itself.

The Sanskrit definitions actually directly relate to the Ancient Chem. Nothingness, Amenet Amen, is the essence from which Ra, Yang Life Force and Raet, Ying Life Force, comes. Thus *the empty/emptiness* and *motion* are represented.

No, zero, Hieroglyphic Letters are stagnant. They are Divine Words with living purposeful energy to inspire the senses, life and living.

Tied into the above paragraph, O has a **connoted** meaning of *From* and *Of*; as ALL life comes Of/From the Hidden Supreme Being, Subjective Being. In the Language of Chem the denoted forms of *From* and *Of* are *Em* and *En*, and ⁓⁓⁓⁓⁓.

For Em, the *Of* is associated with earthly materials comparable to all activities of owls.

The En is linked to the primordial (Of/From/Before the Beginning) waters of Nūt Nū. Thus the En is used in reference to celestial Beings: persons, places and things (Including Angels and Angles), True Self.

CHAPTER 12: Identifying Identity

If a person does not know their name, ethnic cultural background, true color of skin, eye and hair color and temperament, genetic lineage, internal chemical balance or lack thereof, the general energy with which they are greeted by people, strengths and limitations, sexual orientation, gender and gender role, family friends and foes, aspirations, deterrents and such; that person is at a loss in so many stratified ways.

It is safe to say that "Knowledge of Self" relates to many of the above mentioned people, places and things. Yet it is not safe to say that all of those things mentioned are common knowledge to an individual, nor ever known by some.

Something as simple as a name can play a major or seemingly insignificant role in a person's life.

Even so, what is a name? At its basic value it is a label that is spoken and written. In Ren Chem En Metu Neter it is a divine energy.

Therefore the Ancient Egyptian classical practice was to aptly label/name individual Beings. And when it came to naming that which they were intimately concerned about, they were very meticulous.

Meticulousness kindred to Chem seems at present day to be given a back seat for commercial flash appeal. Those who take on cultural names of the ancient Africans seem less aware and even weary of the ancestral cultural energy they are "embracing."

Hypocritically they argue and defend the sanctity of the divine awareness of Chem and Divine Words, but do not engage in serious detailed time consuming study; It is not worth their time to do so, to make so.

Caught up in at times innocent ignore-ance (As they have been misled by so called teachers and experts), they have no knowledge about the depth of variation in philosophy and practice that existed in Ancient Egypt over tens of years to the next 10, to 100 years to the next thousands; from 10,000+ BCE – present.

Errantly they take on a name of which they know little to none of its historical psychosocial value. Furthermore, they take up practices that they believe to be organic to the classical, best of Chem, but are not.

They do things like call themselves Gods and Goddesses, not knowing from where that application came nor its ramifications, and think they are in line with the Universal credo, "Know Thyself."

In his book <u>The Gods of the Egyptians</u> (G.O.E.) [First print 1902, Vol 1, p 4], Wallis Budge writes:

> It is very unfortunate that the animals and the spirits of natural objects, as well as powers of nature were all grouped together by the Egyptians and were described by the word Neteru, which, with considerable inexactness, we are obliged to translate by [or as] gods.

Context is that almost 70 years after Champollion deciphered the Rashit, Budge's writings were some of the first impressions upon the world about Chem, from actual literature from Ancient Egyptians, 2000 – 10,000+ BCE, themselves.

It was for certain the first mass produced transliterations and translations, late 1800s – start of the 1900s.

Oddly he felt "obliged" (Compelled, forced, required, obligated...) to translate Neteru as "gods" for lack of a better word.

He said it was "unfortunate" that the Ancient Egyptians grouped all things natural under such heading.

He continued the topic on pp 63, 68:

We have already said above that the common word given to God, and god, and spirits of every kind, and beings of all sorts, and kinds, and forms, which was supposed to possess any superhuman or supernatural power, Neter... [T]he plural is [Neteru]...

[Relative to Neter being equivalent to the Latin term *Natura* Budge stated,] It need hardly be that there is no good grounds for such an assertion, and it is difficult to see how the eminent Egyptologist could attempt to compare the conceptions of God by a half-civilized African people with those of such cultured nations as the Greeks and Romans.

Granted it was not until 1920, eighteen years later, that his book <u>Egyptian Hieroglyphic Dictionary</u> came out with the many detailed variations, detailed facets, of the term Neter and Netcher.

However the fact that he would malign the Greek and Roman actual ***parent culture,*** which showed obvious external material, intellectual and spiritual advancements that far exceeded their "children's," is sadly ignorant or maliciously intended.

Withstanding, the Chem term Netcher is the etymological archetype for Nature [Nātcher] and Neter for Neuter (Ne[u]ter).

Additionally the term ***god*** (*German:* ***Gott*** *[****Goth***, ***Visigoth***, *Germanic self-proclaimed chosen ones], Proto-Germanic:* ***Guthan***, *Proto-Indo-European:* ***Ghut*** *[Invoke, call], Hebrew/Canaanite:* ***Hod/Ghod*** *[The messenger angel, "door" keeper, way opener/closer, thoughts, mercurial energy...], Sanskrit:* ***Huta*** *[Invoked, called, chosen] and Chem:* ***Hut*** *[Hoot] {Inspire, Enflame, Offering, Invocation/Evocation}*) in the <u>connoted</u> (*Culturally or societally implied*) refers to Supreme Being, but denoted (*Actual meaning*) is **limited** to <u>only one</u> aspect of Supreme Being, Netcher, Nature, The All.

As it may loosely be linked to the Supreme Being or supreme being, it actually speaks of a caller, messenger, "gate" keeper (door man or woman).

It was made famous and pushed by Budge, backed by the British government (Parliament and Crown) and European league of Academia, which hold conferences on such matters on a yearly and more basis.

When the so called cultivated (Awake, Conscious, Conscientious) refer to themselves as Gods and Goddesses or gods and goddesses, they are calling themselves messengers or door keeps. That's great if that is the intent of their exclamations. Not so much so if making reference to the Highest Power of their *Self*.

If one feels compelled with the need to refer to their person as essentially *The All*, all one need say or write is the Chem: *Neter, Netcher* or English: *Neuter, Nature* or the like derivative (Ex: ***I am Nature***), without gaudy vainly asinine alluded to fantasy.

In showing further ignorance or malicious intent (It is unclear which appropriately applies to him) Budge stated on pages 4 – 5 of G.O.E. Vol. 1 that the Ancient Egyptians clearly believed in monotheism (As illustrated by use of Neter and Neteru), but only had such an all-inclusive "grouping" due to the poor limitations of their language.

Further he writes that other "nations of antiquity" found ways out of such a problem by the use of Angels and such. This is oxymoronically after he already wrote that the Chem scribe-priests had a classification system of "Higher" and "Lower" Neteru, aspects of Neter.

That many and all things come from one Supreme Being is the very definition of monotheism, where as anything other than that is hypocritical polytheism, such as the Greek and Roman ways; which shows that the child-cultures misunderstood their "parent."

Fact of the matter is that archetype Chem *metaphysical* so called *angels* are a codification system related to *physical angles*, numbers, degrees, vibrations, words.

In correspondence to Neter/Netcher one of the major ways of delineating or labeling The Neuter's/Nature's key aspects is in citing the origin from which it came, Amenet Amen.

Linguistically AMENETAMEN and Amenet Amen are different forms of the same entity because the pictorial longer more detailed form of writing, Hieroglyphics, had no such concept as small versus "capital" letters.

Neither did the Hieratic shorter picture form, nor Demotic even shorter picture script, have such a system of giving value of one letter over another.

All writing was considered METU NETER (MEDU NEDER), *Of Heated (Fresh) Nourishing Expansions of Nature.*

The concept of hierarchy of letters seemed to develop with the last direct evolution of Hieroglyphics; Coptic; the forbearer of Greek, Etruscan, Canaanite/Phoenician, Roman, Sanskrit and more all the way to this present "*stick figure picture writing*" called *Letters.*

Lttres are nto difnret rfom pcitrues ohtre iwse uyo owuld nto ∂ɞʇ the message written in the first half of this sentence.

Though *poorly drawn* according to written Standard English, it can be generally easily deciphered because it is visually or pictorially recognizable. The pictures/stick figures/letters are discombobulated in order and some are up side down.

Still, the actively cognitive (Ra) portion of our psyche works with the passive cognitive stored memory (Raet) to make sense of the writing, pictorial marks that represent sounds and ideas. Pictures can be understood forwards, backwards, upside down and more.

Whether the picture is long form and detailed or short form and basic, it is writing when the forms come from a standard code of meaning such as Metu Neter or its dialects, offspring.

Thus in Chem all writing was and is sacred representation of language, RAEN (RN/REN) CHEM, *Expansions of Life Force via Chem.*

Actually, AMENETAMEN written Amenet Amen means different things in Chemitic, and English.

The first way of writing the idea shows that all the letters are of equal value in greatness of meaning (Capital) and AMENET and AMEN are one word, one entity with two polarities of Nothingness from which All things come.

The second version relays that Amenet and Amen are **Proper Nouns** and inferred/presupposed as two separate things, her here and him over there (*Proper Nouns have the first letter capital when in the midst of a sentence, or "You Understand" a word is a name/proper noun when at the start of a sentence*).

In the original Chem language the female aspect of a word was not separated from the male, unless specifically making reference to a male or female, yang or yin entity; not speaking of both with one or the other form covering for the other.

Infused in this format is the ideology that all things, female/male/neuter, are always connected, one with many expressions of oneness.

Present day English does not give adequate attention to the masculine, feminine and neuter aspects of words as Spanish, French and some other Latin based, Alphabet derived dialects do.

With Old English writers and *right-ers* (Linguistically orthodox protestant practitioners) especially gave attention to such pen, pencil and paint details.

As the "educated" teachers and students of Old English knew the differences in the specific adjective endings (suffixes), they no doubt knew the potential of excluding such gender specific elements from writing and general societal understanding.

Taken further, it is simple to see how a statement such as "God he…" would be an intentional control device misused (ab-used) by a male dominated perspective, whether it be a woman or man providing that abusive perspective.

As in Spanish it is a telling example that the word Dios (*-o* is the masculine suffix/article) is translated and transliterated as Gods, and Dias (*-a* is the feminine article) is translated and transliterated as meaning Days.

The suffix *–s* renders each of the words plural, so the meaning of both words should be ***Gods feminine (Dias)/Gods masculine (Dios), or Days feminine (Dias)/Days masculine (Dios)***, but not two different definitions for each gender specific form of the same word. Few Spanish speakers are truly aware of what they are doing and saying in the statements, "A Dios (Adios)" and "Buenas Dias."

Put another way when there is plurality (2 or more) and a mixture of female and male, the masculine (male) form of the plural word is used to represent the male and female (I.e. Pad**re** = Father, Mad**re** = Mother, **Padres = Father and Mother** (*Parents*) **or Fathers**).

This is common throughout the Hispanic language and culture.

With French this continues. "Some activist claim that with its persistent use of genders, French is a *sexist* language and should modernize... In French grammar, the masculine form prevails over the feminine form – due to a seventeenth century belief that the masculine was nobler" ("3 unbelievable reasons the French language is the most controversial," Judy McMahon, November 18, 2014).

Ger***man*** has the samular issue; "Men are always classified properly; women almost never. For in our language, the following rule obtains: 99 women singer[s] (i.e. **Sängerinnen**) and one male singer (i.e. **Sänger**) are together 100 singer[s] (i.e. **Sänger**). Gone are the 99 women, not to be found, vanished into a masculine pigeonhole" ("Allen Menschen werden Schwestern," Luise F. Pusch, 1990).

In her book, Communicating Gender, Suzanne Romaine gives a brief history of how the English language became male dominated (pp 65 – 90).

Yet a brief history does not do full justice and persons who claim that the Latin based languages became "sexist" in the 17th century. They miss much of "his" story within history and a lot more of "hers," the female story.

17th Century is 1601 – 1700 CE. The change of gender related suffixes came between the Coptic and Greek and other writings around 2000 – 1500 B.C.E.

Such examples extend throughout unorthodoxly patriarchal (male restrictive) language patterns. It needs to be re-cognized and fixed towards balance between women and men in words (Verbal thought actions) and actions.

It is personally demeaning; disrespectful; to mothers, sisters, daughters, cousins, wives, friends, associates (anyone or anything feminine) to speak words of misplaced male oriented verbal oppression through *codified male dominant language.*

So why should it matter if people refer to God as God He..., or as God or Goddess She?

If God, the Supreme Being is omnipresent (Present in all things), omniscient (Knowledgeable of all things) and omni-potent (All powerful); why verbally **limit the personification** of "God" as a she or he?

Isn't that making incorrect, false, vane (Selfish) images of "God?"

In fact Amen is the neuter form of the term, wrongly used to take the place of the masculine form Amenf of Amenef.

But additionally why do people make statements like, "My God is...?" If there is only One Supreme original Creator? Isn't *It* the God/Higher Power/Supreme Being of all of us *without personal ownership*?

Now that *the word is out*, it's time to give linguistically proper respect to women and men, as men can not gain rightly proportional respect unless *his* complementary counterpart, women, are properly respected as well; Also is the need to give more correct respect and attention to thoughts (Thought-actions), unspoken words.

In the original and classical language of Chem (More ancient than the dynastic periods), Universal understanding and reflection of speech and actions was held critically important towards inner and outer balance and such things were duly noted.

Budge writes, "As to their antiquity there is no room for doubt... [I]t is quite clear, from the way in which they [Female aspects/counterparts] are mentioned, that they represent traditional ideas of an extremely ancient character. One proof of this is the careful mention of the female counterparts of the four great primeval gods, for it is **usual** in the case of the gods who were products of the **purely dynastic** period to **pay small attention** to the goddesses who were regarded as their wives (p 287)."

Budge then gives examples of some major counterparts that represent two complementary "opposites" of one Being.

1st, "...[K]nown to the Egyptians in very early times were AMEN [Amenef] and his consort AMEN[E]T..." "...[who] numbered among the primeval [aspects of Neter (Nature)]..." (Gods of the Egyptian [G.O.E.] Vol. 2, p 1).

Additionally in another of his works he transcribed from sacred papyrus text he relayed, "The [H]idden Circle in the [D]uat wherein this great [Neter] is born; he cometh forth into the pool of **NŪ**, and he taketh his place in the body of **Nūt**" (Egyptian Heaven and Hell, p 258).

That is, The Hidden (Amenet Amen) Universal Nature comes from the Expansion of Inert Energy (NŪ) to be "born" from the Inert Energetic Universal Womb (NŪT).

The following is one way to spell NU with hieroglyphs from Chemit:

Coinciding; the Coptic and Greek letter N is called Nu, which comes from the *Long Form Pictorial hieroglyph.*

Additionally, taking the first "up-down-up" marks of the squiggled line of hieroglyphic NU renders a stick figure bold and "italic" *N (NⱲNⱲN)*.

Budge stated, "Nu was the inert mass of watery matter from which the world was created." (G.O.E., Vol. 1 pp 283 –284). But that was his "European" late 18 – early 1900's male perspective.

Presented in 2022, as was such in pre-dynastic Chem some 6000⁺ years ago, more often is the perspective of giving credit to both female and male counterparts when credit is due. History repeats... A more universal approach, as it is "Nu and Nut from which the world comes."

Without the application of Universal principals, making practical proper use of Metu Neter is like building a pyramid without a 90° angle; It ain't happening.

Theories and arbitrary use of Divine Words is as useless as making paper or stucco pyramids for Hollywood scenes from movies; it may give the form illusion of being real, but in actuality is weak in content and dangerous when perceived by some as being true to life.

Proper identification of people, places and things does not only reside in the external labeling of them; but in proper assessment of internal workings and accurate alignment of the inner with the outer towards optimal expression and comprehension.

Being definitive is a critical part to this.

CHAPTER 13: X Sighting Summary

This is the final chapter of this book. X, Y and Z are the final letters of the English alphabet and of this discourse to be dealt with in a definitive manner.

It is sarcastically funny and truly sad to see most English etymology and general dictionaries *tap dance* around not knowing the origin, thus denoted meaning, of the word/letter X (*eX*).

Quite so because submission to the historical truth of the origin of AlphaBet is the simple resolution to such enigma. The "child culture has gotten lost in the woods, been knocked around too much and suffered a case of amnesia as to whom its parents are and that for which they stood and stand."

Just as much as the parent culture has gone unrecognized related to language, there seems to be a soap opera like *fiend* in the midst that interjects propaganda to keep the "children" from reuniting with the "parents" and claiming their rich inheritance.

Who are the children? All who use AlphaBet based writing in any form. Who are the parents? Chem, Ancient Egypt; Punt, Ancient Sudan; Kush, Ancient Ethiopia; Ancient Nyanza; Ancient South Central Africa.

The mentioned dictionaries are grossly satisfied with stating: 1. X stands for the unknown. 2. X developed from Algebra (Al Geb Ra) around 700 CE (AD). 3. Contradictory to #2, X developed from the Greek Chi [Kai/Ky/Kī] 4. X is used in genetics 5. X refers to multiplication 6. X was used to represent a kiss in the Middle Ages relative to a cross, sincerity.

Nowhere in Mass Media (14 major companies control the media of over 200 countries) is mentioned in major dictionaries that:

1. Ancient Egypt is the oldest documented origin of Al Geb Ra (Algebra) and other genres (Gene Ras) of mathematics.

2. Ancient Africa is the oldest documented origin of a *Cross of any type.*

3. There is no known origin of when exactly Coptic developed as it came directly from Ancient African Egyptian lineage; Coptic did not always refer to Christianity but was first a general reference to Egypt/Qupt/Copt; **As such Ancient Coptic is older than Greek and is Pre-Ancient Greece; X was used in Coptic/Qupt/Egypt thousands of years before Greece**

4. The Hieroglyph of a water lily or lotus pad and its foundational roots with the X like structure representing potential increased growth of many other pads and flowers, ⚍ , has the numerical value of 1000 and sound equivalence to present day X, as in X-ray or hex (hx).

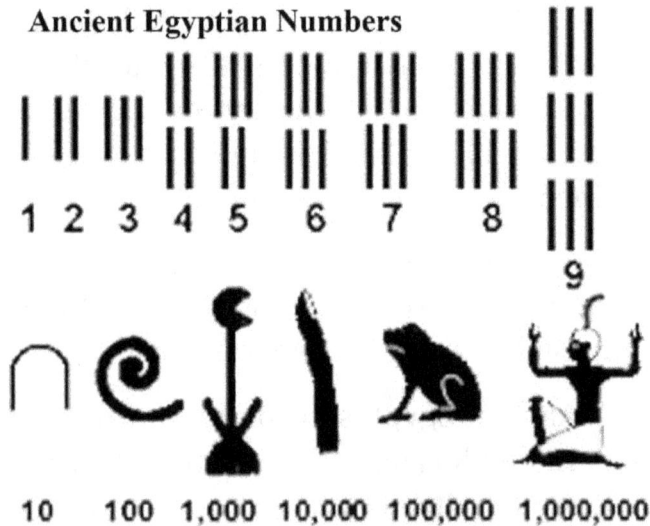

Ancient Egyptian Numbers

1 2 3 4 5 6 7 8 9

10   100 1,000 10,000 100,000 1,000,000

5. The X at the base of the plant roots under water stands for an unknown number of plentiful offshoots, thus 1 multiplied by the infinite.

6. The multiplication from 1 to many offspring is directly linked to genetics.

7. 1 to 1000 references multiplication.

8. This symbol was used 4000+ BCE.

9. The pad foreshadows flowering, multiplying.

It is somewhat baffling why United Nations Educational, Scientific and Cultural Organization (UNESCO); a major portion of the United Nations; fakes ignorance or is actually purposely ignore-ant of the many organic contributions to the world's cultures and languages Africa has made and makes.

They also perpetuate such ignorance by setting restrictive standards of National and International Academic Organizations. They literally accept and push ignorance over truthful education and enlightenment.

It is the responsibility of the general masses to share truth, but how is truth known if not definitively shown? Such is the purpose of this book related to Hieroglyphics. So, seemingly new Glyphs are featured here.

However Hieroglyphs like those shown to stand for X, Y, Z (⚥ , Y , ——◁▷——) and the like have been known by world academic organizations for thousands of years, but either relegated to wasteful redundancy or left out altogether.

Y , Y, is the Hieroglyphic representation of a support beam. The fame of the beam comes from the Chem Creation Story where Neter as Raet Ra sets the four "Pillars of Maat," Maat Maa as the foundation for the Universe and all within it.

Whether it is a metaphysical support or physical is noted by other determinative Hieroglyphs that accompany it.

Its usage is noted in the professional world of Egyptology, even in the Egyptian Hieroglyphic Dictionary by Budge, but its usage is obscure.

That its form is a Y is unmistakable. It has retained its structure and sonic value for over 6000 years. In Spanish Y (Ee) translates as the <u>supportive conjunction</u> *And*, as И (Ee) does the same in Russian.

Unlike in English where it may stand for several different sounds, Ys hieroglyphic codex renders it as y/ie/ee/ē (Linguistical<u>y</u>, Countr<u>ie</u>s, S<u>ee</u>, M<u>e</u>) when there is a vertical dash (Hieroglyphic E) over it and ye/yeh when there is not.

Greek Upsilon, Ipsilon, Ypsilon/Yipsilon (U, I, and Y); like Kappa and Qoppa - K and Q; experienced much confusion and redundancy with use, which spilled over to derivative dialects later.

Phoenician/Canaanite *Waw* (W, Double U) and U (Yew) are thought to have had usage as a Y as well, though there is little actual evidence to prove such.

Copt He (Hee, EE)/Ue (Yew) shows proof in usage as a present day surviving dialect. However depending on what offshoot of Coptic, the training of the writer/scribe and the placement of the letter in a word, the sound varies from EE to Ue to Yeh.

With the high influx of immigrants and emigrants (students and educators) in and out of Ancient Egypt around 2000 – 1500 BCE and on, it is easy to see how details could have gotten contorted when dealing with subtle differences between 3000 or more Hieroglyphs to learn.

However that is one of the major purposes for detailed drawings, to differentiate one from another.

With English, either the reader knows the original intent of the sound and meaning with Y or they do not. What's more is that the writer may not know the true meaning of how (Proper usage) and what (Proper sound) they are writing. Thank god for Hieroglyphs.

The last stick figure Metu Neter in English alphabet is Z.

Usage of the Champollion Formula and the Ameninhat Hieroglyphic Charts yields Coptic Za/Zita/Zeta as the Hieroglyphic door bolts; ***Close out, close in, zip up, zip***.

Sonically closely related to *S*, the *Z* sound is at times represented with a double *S*, *SS*, in English and other dialects; or single *Se*, as with Plea<u>se</u> a variant of Pleas (Plural of *Plea*), and *eeS*, Kn<u>ees</u>, akin to the ending sound of bree<u>ze</u> or ma<u>ze</u>.

Bolting a door obviously relates to closing in or closing out something. This does not mean the door is locked. This does mean that the Ancient Egyptians had doors and bolts to secure closing them.

4000 – 6000 or more BCE when much of the world had no language, cities, towns, housing nor knowledge of how to get or make housing; Chem was flaunting all of that, accessorized with doors and bolts.

In 2022, there are various people and places in 1st, 2nd and 3rd world countries that do not have bolts nor doors, along with no clean washing nor drinking water readily available (Ancient Egyptian priests [Female and Male] were generally taught how to purify the at times rancid waters of the Nile and water in general).

This is not a bragging stance about Chem. People being without clean water is not a topic for uplifting anyone. It is testimony that the science for cleaning water existed over 6000 years ago and today that science has not been shared world-wide. Same holds true for housing the homeless with homes that have doors with bolts.

Nevertheless, Hieroglyphics is the topic here and the Z without redundancy with S is represented as such: ———⬤——— .

Concerning its Canaanite/Phoenician/ Hebrew usage as Za/Zayin the letter is identified as being a sword via connoted representation of fighting for survival, but its denoted meaning of *Subsistence* or *Nourishment* is actually close to the original, as door bolts were used for shelter and granary storage facilities.

A **complementary "opposite"** polarity of *Keeping Something or Someone Safely Enclosed* **is** *Attacking or Forcing Entry* with a *Sword*; and in original Hieroglyphics this would have a determinative added to the *Door Bolts* Glyph alerting the reader that the antithesis (Opposite of safety) is meant.

Perhaps that was the inspiration for the Hebrew stick figure letter Zayin, ⵟ ,that *"looks like a sword* (As stated by Hebrew and other linguists)."

From original Medu Neder, a Z can be made with the hieroglyph for SS/CC rightly placed or via the manipulation of the bolt , , and its development is seen on the AHC.

From ABC to XYZ there is clear evidence of AlphaBet's evolution from Hieroglyphics to English and other Latin based dialects/"languages."

The fact is that no one is writing nor speaking the English Language. We are speaking the English, Spanish, Russian, Hindu... dialects of *Metu Neter En Ren Chem*!

In accepting truth even from an "enemy," (Alan Gardiner was a type of Enemy to Ancient Egyptian literary truth) He was correct stating that Hieroglyphics live on in present day "Western" dialects.

Definitively, Hieroglyphics live on in the "West, North, South and East."

ABCs - 7000+ Years of EVOLUTION Worldwide

SESH MTUNTR Hieroglyphics 3500+ BCE	SESH SHA Hieratic 3200+ BCE	SESH SHA II Demotic 2000+ BCE	Meit N Rem Chemi Coptic 1500+ BCE	KANAANA/CANAAN Phoenician 1500+ BCE	ETRUSCAN RASNA 1000+ BCE	UINE/HELLENE Greek 750+ BCE	Hapiru/IVRIT Hebrew 135- CE	AL ARABYAH Arabic 650- CE	L'ATIN/LATIN English 1000+ BCE
			Λ a			Α α	א or אַ		A a
			Β β			Β β	ב		B b
			C			Σ σ	ד		C
			Λ λ			Δ δ	ד		D d
		Jinkim	-/Є			Ε ε	אַ		E e
			Ϥ ϥ			Φ φ	ם		F f
			Γ ς			Γ γ	ג		G g
						Γ-ξ	ח		G-h
						Ξ ξ	ח		H-h
			Ι			Ι ι	א		I i
			Χ			Υ υ	י		J j
			Κ			Κ	כ		K k
			Λ			Λ λ	ל		L l
			Ⲙ μ			Μ μ	מ		M m
			Ν ⲛ			Ν ν	ן		N n
			Ο			Ο	א		O
			Π π			Π π	פ		P p
			ϭ ϭ			Q	ק		Q q
			Ρρ/Ⲣ			Ρ ρ	ר		R r
			ϛ ⲍ̄			Σ σ	▯ and ▯		S
			Τ τ			Τ τ	▯ and ▯		T t
			Υ ⲅ			Ʊ	▯		U u
			Β β			Β β	ב		V
			Ⲱ ω			ω	ו		W
			Χ			Χ	▯		X
			Η			Υ υ	אַ		Y y
			Υ ⲅ			Υ υ	ו		Y y
			Ζ ⲍ			Ζ ζ	ז		Z

Rich Ameninhat
HIEROGLYPHIC DEFINITIVES

www.ingramcontent.com/pod-product-compliance
Lightning Source LLC
Chambersburg PA
CBHW071534040426
42452CB00008B/1011